Praise for

FAITH, HOPE, LOVE, & DEPLOYMENT

"After 23 years as a military couple, we have faced our share of deployments, long TDYs, short-notice PCSs, and challenging duty assignments. It is a constant battle to not let the demands of our military life create distance or division in our relationship. *Faith, Hope, Love, & Deployment* offers faith-filled encouragement and practical assignments that will not only start the necessary conversations, but will keep them going. Ultimately, this will build connectedness and growth in your marriage. Heather is a skilled writer and her message is delivered with transparency and emotion. Her message is captivating and powerful not because it comes from surviving tragedy, but because her message is *not* one of despair. It is one of faith, of hope, and most of all love."

> —**Brigadier General Tim Gibson,** former commander of the 10th ABW, United States Air Force Academy; **Nancy Gibson,** wife of General Gibson and Air Force Key Spouse Mentor

"The words of Heather Gray are truly inspiring and encouraging! In the midst of dealing with her grief, this Air Force Key Spouse continues to learn from her adversity and uses it to benefit others. Although this book was written for military couples, anyone reading it will gain something to add meaning to their life and to the lives of others."

> —**Mrs. Paula Roy,** wife of retired Chief Master Sergeant of the Air Force and Director of Family Services for the Air Force Association

"Deployment can bring about so many feelings of sadness, loneliness, and anxiety. It can become instinctual to just want to tough it out, but we believe God calls us to flourish and thrive throughout this spiritual journey. This devotional can be just the tool a couple needs to make this spiritual journey together in a time when it is so easy to become disconnected from each other and from God. Heather's devotional walks you week by week through topics that are extremely relevant to the spiritual and emotional issues that can arise during deployment. By engaging with your spouse through this devotional, going deeper into God's word, and reflecting on topics so relevant to military families, this time of separation can be one in which you learn to rely more fully on

God. Make a plan to work through this devotional with your spouse, and see the ways God can grow each of your hearts, even when you're oceans apart."

—**Sgt. Christopher and Lauren Schoate,** U.S. Army

"Faith, Hope, and Love . . . the epitome of how the Gray's lived every aspect of their lives. This devotional is what military couples have needed for years. Through David and Heather's story, readers will be encouraged to press into Christ through every challenge faced during deployment. Our lives have been personally blessed by their influence and enriched by their Christian example. We pray that this book will act as a vessel to positively impact military marriages!"

—**Major and Mrs. Andrew Hunter,** U.S. Air Force

"Heather Gray has served many roles in her life . . . devoted wife, loving mother of three, a strong believer, and now survivor. She is on a new journey to lend support to military couples of all ranks with her remarkable devotional. I wish my wife Jody and I would have had access to such an insightful devotional years ago; it will be a tremendous benefit to all husbands and wives, as well as those who are engaged. These forty devotions will enable couples to draw closer to God, closer to one another, improve communications inside the marriage and family, and improve the foundation of a biblically based relationship. I'm confident your marriage will gain greater strength and meaning from this timely and inspirational work."

—**Richard Y. Newton III,** retired Lieutenant General, U.S. Air Force

"This devotional by Heather Gray is the answer to hundreds of unvoiced prayers. Only someone who's walked the path of separation because of war can write the words penned in this devotional for military couples. The honesty and faith found in the pages will bring comfort to military families who find themselves in similar circumstances. The author points the path to intimacy with the Lord and with each other, no matter the physical miles that lie between them."

—**Edie Melson,** military family blogger for Guideposts.com, and author of *Fighting Fear: Winning the War at Home When Your Soldier Leaves for Battle*

FAITH, HOPE, LOVE, & DEPLOYMENT

FAITH, HOPE, LOVE, & DEPLOYMENT

40 DEVOTIONS FOR MILITARY COUPLES

HEATHER GRAY

LEAFWOOD
PUBLISHERS

Faith, Hope, Love, & Deployment
40 Devotions for Military Couples

LEAFWOOD
PUBLISHERS

Copyright © 2014 by Heather Gray

ISBN 978-0-89112-612-6
Printed in the United States of America

Published in association with The Blythe Daniel Agency, Inc., PO Box 64197, Colorado Springs, CO 80962.

Cover design by Thinkpen Design, LLC | Interior text design by Sandy Armstrong

Photo on Dedication page used by permission of Sublime Studios. Author photo on back cover used by permission of Courtney Sanchez.

For information, contact:
Abilene Christian University Press | 1626 Campus Court | Abilene, Texas 79601
1-877-816-4455 | www.leafwoodpublishers.com

18 19 / 7 6 5 4 3

In memory of my beloved David . . .
the embodiment of faith, hope, and love.

"This is how we know what love is: Jesus Christ laid down his life for us.
And we ought to lay down our lives for our brothers and sisters"
(1 JOHN 3:16).

For the men and women in uniform who defend our freedom
and for their families who also serve.

Heather and Major David Gray

TABLE OF CONTENTS

ACKNOWLEDGMENTS

First and foremost, I must give all credit to the Author of all, whose redemptive blood provides for every good thing.

Thank you to my children, Nyah, Garrett, and Ava, for your never-ending love and support. Your resiliency inspires me. I love you all.

Thank you to General and Mrs. Shelton for catching a vision for this project and connecting me with the support and resources I needed to take it on.

Chaplain Viccellio, "Chaps," you've stuck with me from our brainstorming session in the old BX (base exchange) all the way to completion over a year and a half later. Your tireless encouragement, feedback, insight, and prayers were invaluable to me. Thank you.

Blythe Daniel, thank you for being willing to take a chance on me. Having an agent made me feel like writing might actually be a valid way to spend my time!

Thank you to my friends and family for the behind-the-scenes work you did to help me accomplish this. You invested countless hours of babysitting, helped with homeschool, shared meals, offered feedback, cried with me, kept the tea flowing, and filled me with encouraging words. I honestly couldn't have seen this to fruition without all of you.

And finally, thanks to Leafwood Publishers for bringing to life the vision my husband and I had when we started working on this together during his last deployment. It has been a pleasure working with such amazing people.

FOREWORD

I first met Heather Gray during the summer of 2012. She and her husband, David, were beginning a book to help couples during deployments and wanted a chaplain's feedback on their devotionals. I was immediately impressed by this young, energetic, and faith-filled woman. Her devotions reflected a rare passion for God, the military family, and the stress of separation.

Then IT happened. On a Wednesday in August 2012, I received a text early in the morning: "Chaps, I don't know any way to say this other than David was killed yesterday by a suicide bomber."

Overwhelmed by the news, I began to question God. "Are you kidding me? Heather is writing a book to help downrange marriages and you allow this to happen?" Life is mysterious as are the ways of God. I thought, "How will she ever finish this book?"

Today, Heather's passion for God and the military family is stronger than ever. Her writing is simple, beautiful, and profound. She reveals her indomitable Faith, her never-ending Hope, and her tender Love for God and his military families. *Faith, Hope, Love, & Deployment* is a new resource for the deployed family. Its tough and tender approach challenges couples to go deeper in their relationship even when separated. Insightful and practical, this book of devotions is a must-do for the deployed marriage and will be valuable to all military couples.

Ch., Lt. Col. Hodges Viccellio, USAF

INTRODUCTION

If you are looking for a book written by an expert with a PhD that will give you clinical knowledge on how to better your military marriage, you should look elsewhere. If you are looking for a candid collection of personal stories, Scripture, and practical advice gained from experience, this is for you.

Faith, Hope, Love, & Deployment was born from what my husband and I considered necessity. We wanted something to keep communication open, draw us closer to the Lord and each other, and challenge us to dig into the Word . . . all while he was deployed. And I personally felt that handwritten letters were a lost art. I wanted the stack of letters from abroad, tied together with a ribbon like the treasure troves of past generations. Sadly, my husband was killed in action halfway through writing this book. I was left with few—but precious—letters, one of which I received on the day of his funeral. It was in response to a question posed on the topic of patriotism. He was asked to write a letter explaining why he was willing to lay his life on the line for his country. At a time when that very question swirled in my head, it was a balm to my aching heart to have it answered in his own handwriting. I knew then the value of what we had endeavored, and vowed by the grace of God to finish what we had started.

It is my prayer that you, too, will benefit from *Faith, Hope, Love, & Deployment*. The book is broken down into forty devotions. Each one stands alone so you won't feel overwhelmed by trying to keep up with homework from week to week. You can do them in any order. Although the activities can certainly be done at any time, if you are getting this book before the deployment begins and you have children, I would recommend doing the topic entitled "Children" before departure.

Each devotion has four components. **Faith**: Scripture memory verses for him and her (all verses are from the 2011 NIV translation unless otherwise noted). **Hope**: first-person narrative and insight from eleven years as a Christian military couple along with conversation starters and reflection questions that can be done all at once or daily. **Love**: a guided letter-writing assignment. **Deployment**: practical tips, resources, and encouragement for making the best of this time of separation.

I recommend you have a journal dedicated to the work you will do through this time. You will often find me asking you to make lists, be intentionally observant, and record your findings. It will be easier if you keep them together in one place. When your deployment is over, that journal will provide you with tangible evidence of how God worked in your life and marriage during a difficult time. I guarantee you will refer back to it as a reminder of his faithfulness.

I hope you will be as blessed in doing this together as we were in writing it. The most important thing is that you keep communication open and be honest with one another throughout the process. This is likely to open doors to conversations you've wanted to have but perhaps never felt comfortable with or have not found the time to initiate. Embrace the opportunity to take your marriage and your relationship with the Lord to a deeper level by engaging in all areas covered in this book.

And remember, "These three remain: faith, hope and love. But the greatest of these is love" (1 Cor. 13:13).

1

SEPARATION

"True love doesn't mean being inseparable,
it means being separated and nothing changes."

—Anonymous

FAITH

Him: "[W]hen we were orphaned by being separated from you for a short time (in person, not in thought), out of our intense longing we made every effort to see you. . . . Indeed, you are our glory and joy" (1 Thess. 2:17, 20).

Her: "May the Lord keep watch between you and me when we are away from each other" (Gen. 31:49b).

HOPE

Forget Disney World. An airport terminal on the day of a soldier's homecoming is the happiest place on earth. But rewind to the beginning of a deployment, and there is nothing more gut-wrenching than that same terminal. Separation hurts regardless of how many times you go through it or how long it lasts.

It begins as a baby . . . commonly called separation anxiety. A child whose brain is too immature to understand object permanence becomes very upset when he is separated from the one he loves most. As we grow up, we learn that the majority of that distress is without merit and therefore irrational. While separation is uncomfortable, it in itself will not cause permanent damage. But that doesn't mean the aching feeling it brings doesn't feel debilitating at times.

More times than I'd like to remember I have watched my children cling to their daddy as if life ends the moment they let go. Their little hearts break every time, and I'm left wondering how I'm to put the pieces back together when my own is broken as well. Yet no matter how often I bring the fragments to my Savior, "he heals the brokenhearted and binds up [my] wounds" (Ps. 147:3).

Then the news came of our first year-long deployment. I immediately doubted that even God had enough tape and glue to hold us together for that long. We Air Force folks are spoiled by deployments lasting typically no longer than six months. But the Lord prompted me to prepare my heart. If a marriage is made up of just a husband and wife, when one of the components is removed, the other will likely fall. But "a cord of three strands is not quickly broken" (Eccles. 4:12b).

It isn't that God is unwilling to piece our hearts back together later—it's that he is ready to show us how to prevent separation from breaking them.

Conversation Starters/Reflection Questions: **Separation**

1. Can you think of a time in your life when you were lost or separated from a loved one? How did you cope then?

2. Have you ever had to give up something of value? If so, how did you cope?

3. Do you think it is possible to be physically separated and have nothing in your relationship change? Why or why not?

4. How do you hope this separation will grow your marriage?

5. Does absence really make the heart grow fonder? How so? Or why not?

LOVE

Write a letter to your spouse that expresses how much you are going to miss him or her during this time of separation.

_____

_____

_____

_____

_____

_____

_____

_____

_____

_____

_____

_____

_____

_____

_____

_____

_____

DEPLOYMENT

As much as possible this week (via text, email, FaceTime, etc.), tell your spouse specific things you miss about him or her when you're not together. Work on becoming more intentional about expressing your longing for your spouse during this time of separation.

2

ANXIETY

*"Anxiety does not empty tomorrow of its sorrows,
but only empties today of its strength."*

—CHARLES SPURGEON, *pastor and author*

FAITH

Him: "Anxiety in a man's heart weighs it down, but a good word makes
it glad" (Prov. 12:25 NASB).

Her: "Be anxious for nothing, but in everything by prayer and suppli-
cation with thanksgiving let your requests be made known to God"
(Phil. 4:6 NASB).

HOPE

"Don't be alarmed. When you come through the gate, there's going to
be a guy on top of a Humvee with a big gun pointed at you."

These were the words my husband spoke to me over the phone
as I sat in line waiting to enter the gates of the military installation
I was supposed to call home. It was September 13, 2001. I had been
married four weeks and three days and was already questioning what
I had gotten myself into. Granted, 9/11 had changed the way even sea-
soned military families went about life. But this didn't change the fact

that I was embarking on a journey about which I knew nothing and for which I felt completely unprepared. The anxiety that welled inside me threatened, more than once, to blossom into full-blown panic. I had to practice turning all my anxious thoughts into prayer requests in order to keep it from doing so.

Fast-forward to the end of our military career—being handed a folded flag and hearing the words "on behalf of a grateful nation." That same anxiety welled up again and I found myself gasping for air. But don't let my reference to the military's occupational hazard scare you away. Let it encourage you that even in the worst-case scenario God will sustain you. Anxiety occurs when we hold on to our troubles, our stress, or our difficult situations and refuse to turn them over to the Lord. He is far more capable of carrying our burdens for us than we are.

In this week's Scripture, we are told to be anxious for nothing. There are times this feels impossible. Especially during deployment. The uncertainty of your spouse's safety is just one example of what might weigh heavy on the minds of both husband and wife. But don't be afraid to take *everything* to the Lord in prayer. Nothing is too small a concern. If it's important to you, it's important to your Savior.

Try to remember that an anxious heart leaves little room for the joy the Lord has to offer. Ask God to help you see things from his point of view. When you learn to see it from a different perspective, the menacing guy on the Humvee becomes the armed guard protecting your home.

Conversation Starters/Reflection Questions: **Anxiety**

1. What is the difference between anxiety, anticipation, and fear?

2. Is it possible to "be anxious for nothing"? If yes, how?

3. Share a time when you were anxious about something. What did it feel like? How did you respond? How was the situation resolved?

4. What makes you most anxious? What excites you most? How can you turn anxiety into excitement?

5. If an anxious heart robs you of your present joy, what can a glad heart, filled with excitement, do?

LOVE

Write a reassuring letter to your spouse that encourages giving all anxiety to the Lord.

DEPLOYMENT

This week's memory verse implores us to offer "a good word." Brainstorm possible sources of anxiety during deployment. Make a specific list. Leave room beside each entry so that you can write the antithesis. Arming yourself with countermeasures will enable you or your spouse to offer "a good word" when anxiety threatens to seize your heart.

3

LONELINESS

"Pray that your loneliness may spur you into finding something to live for, great enough to die for."

—Dag Hammarskjöld, *Secretary-General of the United Nations, 1953–1961*

FAITH

Him: "No one will be able to stand against you all the days of your life. As I was with Moses, so I will be with you; I will never leave you nor forsake you" (Josh. 1:5).

Her: "And surely I am with you always, to the very end of the age" (Matt. 28:20b).

HOPE

It was the night of my son's end-of-year school program. My husband had been deployed for about a month and a half. I arrived early with my other two children in tow so I could save enough room for my friends to sit with us as well. The room filled with families toting video cameras and tripods. A dad in a flight suit sat down directly in front of us. My youngest looked up at me, hugging her "daddy doll" (a small pillow bearing the image of my husband) and said, "I wonder if he's seen daddy at work." I took a deep breath and pulled her in close.

With no family nearby, I had invited our neighbors to join us and was looking forward to the company. Checking my phone to see if they needed directions, I discovered a text message that something had come up and they weren't going to make it. A twinge of loneliness kicked me. I took another deep breath and decided not to let it get to me. Plenty of people do the single parent thing all the time, I reasoned.

Just then a friend and her husband walked in. Perking up, I decided to invite them to fill the empty space next to us. When I offered the spots we had saved, she flashed an apologetic smile and told me her family had already saved seats somewhere else. She was polite and offered for us to sit with them, but the lights dimmed and they scurried to their seats. I was grateful it was dark because tears of loneliness streamed down my face, despite my best efforts to hold them in.

Of all the struggles deployment brings, I think loneliness is one of the most difficult to swallow. All I can do is offer a few suggestions. First, try to be aware of others' needs instead of dwelling on what you lack. How much are you pouring into those around you? The person sitting next to you at the deployed spouses' dinner or the soldier in front of you in the convoy might be feeling just as lonely as you are. Be intentional about community.

And second, remember you are never truly alone. Psalm 139:2 (NLT) says, "You know when I sit down or stand up. You know my thoughts even when I'm far away." God knows us, loves us, and hears our cries. When the lights dim and the darkness closes in, seek him and you'll never be lonely.

Conversation Starters/Reflection Questions: **Loneliness**

1. Would you describe yourself as a "loner" or a "people person"? How would you describe your spouse?

2. What are some practical ways you can combat loneliness during deployment?

3. What do you think it means to bear one another's burdens?

4. Do you think loneliness is caused by being without human contact, or can you be lonely in a room full of people?

5. What are some ways God can use loneliness to draw you closer to him and to each other?

LOVE

Write a letter to your spouse in which you remind him (or her) that he is never alone because he (or she) carries your love with him always.

DEPLOYMENT

Make a list of things you might say to your spouse if he or she were heading into a party or military function knowing no one, or perhaps into a long night mission. Feed these to your spouse as feelings of loneliness creep in.

4

COMMUNITY

*"One of the deepest forms of poverty a person
can experience is isolation. . . . It is not by isolation
that man establishes his worth, but by placing himself
in relation with others and with God."*

—POPE BENEDICT XVI

FAITH

Him: "And let us consider how we may spur one another on toward love
and good deeds, not giving up meeting together, as some are in the habit
of doing, but encouraging one another—and all the more as you see the
Day approaching" (Heb. 10:24–25).

Her: "The righteous choose their friends carefully" (Prov. 12:26a).

HOPE

When David was training for special forces, they did an exercise called
buddy breathing. Two people are submerged in water with one snorkel
or, in deep water, one dive tank. They link arms to stay connected, and
one person takes a breath through the snorkel or valve and then passes
it to the other. This is actually harder than it sounds. If the partners
don't work together to synchronize the timing of their breaths and trust

one another completely, panic sets in and the situation goes downhill very quickly.

The same concept is true within the fellowship of believers. We jump into the water of life circumstances thinking we've got our situation handled. Especially during deployment, it is easy to isolate yourself and go into survival mode on your own. Whether you're the one at home or downrange, sometimes it feels easier just to retreat into yourself and not reach out to others. But when the seas become stormy and we start taking on water, we rapidly conclude we cannot do this alone. And isolation is not God's design for us anyway. He didn't equip any one person with everything necessary for survival. He distributed different gifts throughout the body of believers for a purpose.

The Spirit of the Lord has many faces. He can be seen in unique ways when we spend time in community. He put all of us on this planet together. If we forsake the fellowship of believers, we miss out on opportunities to see the thread of his presence woven throughout us all.

But sometimes he woos us to a valley . . . such as deployment. And in that valley, it can be difficult to realize we aren't alone. It's even harder when sometimes God himself feels distant. But I'm learning that when I can't experience him personally or recognize that he's still moving in my life, he is still present. I can see him in the face of my son's football coach who volunteers his time to pour into young lives. I can hear him in the voice of a dear friend who cared enough to boldly tell me I was so caught up in what I've lost that I have forgotten how much I am still loved. I can feel him in the hugs of a dozen college students who gave up their Saturday night to encourage me and the kids. And his fingerprints are all over the little hands that hold mine as we navigate this present darkness together. So I will cling to the promise that his Word is true.

"Therefore I am now going to allure her; I will lead her into the wilderness and speak tenderly to her" (Hosea 2:14). He doesn't lead us to the desert just to abandon us there. He leads us to a place stripped of ourselves so that we can better hear his voice and recognize the earthly model of a relationship with him. The bride of Christ. The fellowship of believers.

We can't save each other. Only he can do that. But as we wait for his return, we wait together. As we go through the hard times that the military life brings, we must jump into the water and buddy breathe until rescue comes.

Conversation Starters/Reflection Questions: **Community**

1. Why do you think religion and politics are considered taboo conversation topics in some communities?

2. Why do you think it's important not to forsake the fellowship of believers, especially during deployment?

3. How can the deployed spouse find a fellowship of believers while downrange?

4. In what ways are you plugging into your church community both to serve and be served?

5. Why is it important to continue to share your faith and belief in Christ with others, even in the midst of difficult circumstances?

LOVE

Write a letter to your spouse recalling a time you felt you were a vital part of a biblical community and how it was beneficial.

DEPLOYMENT

Positive, encouraging relationships with fellow Christians are vital to sustaining oneself during separation. Discuss what the "fellowship of believers" looks like for each of you during deployment. With whom are you choosing to spend your time? Brainstorm together a list of ways that each of you is serving and allowing others to serve you. Pray together over your friends, co-workers, neighbors, and others in your sphere of influence.

5

BOUNDARIES

"Good fences make good neighbors."

—Robert Frost, *American poet*

FAITH

Him: "Do to others as you would have them do to you" (Luke 6:31).

Her: "Above all else, guard your heart, for everything you do flows from it" (Prov. 4:23).

HOPE

A sense of urgency enveloped me as I could see nothing but the problems and hardships surrounding me. I was buying into the enemy's lies that no one cared and I had been wronged beyond repair. Late one night, my emotions got the better of me, and I group texted my pastor, the elders, and their wives. Multiple times. While I thought I was acting within proper boundaries—not addressing a man without his wife—I still wasn't respecting their boundaries because I wasn't respecting their time . . . or data usage! They wisely ignored me, and the next day one of the women put the pieces of my broken ego back together, and the issue was handled properly.

In their book *Boundaries,* Henry Cloud and John Townsend say, "Any confusion of responsibility and ownership in our lives is a problem of boundaries." They go on to say, "Many clinical psychological symptoms, such as depression, anxiety disorders, eating disorders, addictions, impulsive disorders, guilt problems, shame issues, panic disorders, and marital and relational struggles, find their root in conflicts with boundaries."[1]

While having appropriate boundaries with people of the opposite sex is vitally important to protecting your marriage, boundaries can be so much more than that. They are about respecting another person's time and space. This idea is sometimes contrary to the well-intentioned notion that says, "Don't let the sun go down on your anger." Many times I have subscribed to that very thinking. My tendency is to take on the attitude that "if it's important we will resolve it now, at all costs, no matter how ugly it gets along the way." But that is not the heart condition we are called to hold.

We must examine every action with Scripture as a reference, seek godly counsel before confronting, and make allowances for the boundaries others have placed in their lives.

Having said that, I can scarcely think of a time when boundaries are more important to establish than during deployment. The extended absence of your spouse poses the potential for the lines of appropriate behavior to become blurred. You are under greater stress as you face alone things you would usually do together. There is a lesser degree of accountability to maintain the standard of conduct that you know your spouse expects. Having to depend on many outside sources instead of each other creates a tendency to forget that others also have boundaries of which you must be aware.

But remember, Psalm 139:5 says, "You hem me in behind and before, and you lay your hand upon me." You are not alone in the pursuit of the path of righteousness. Allow God to be the hedge of protection around you.

Conversation Starters/Reflection Questions: **Boundaries**

1. Define *boundaries*.

2. Do you feel you are good at establishing and keeping appropriate boundaries with your spouse? With others? If not, what needs to be done?

3. Can trying to control what other people think about you or how they respond to a situation constitute crossing boundaries? If yes, why?

4. Who is the first person you go to when you are upset, happy, etc.?

5. Describe a time when someone did not respect your boundaries. Explain how it made you feel and how you handled it.

LOVE

Write a letter to your spouse declaring all the reasons he or she is your best friend. Express a commitment to becoming aware of the boundaries even within that relationship.

_____

_____

_____

_____

_____

_____

_____

_____

_____

_____

_____

_____

DEPLOYMENT

Sometimes extended separation requires spouses to depend more heavily on others than on each other. Identify tendencies within your current situation, downrange and at home, that pose the potential for inappropriate behavior. Remember that boundaries don't just include interaction with the opposite sex. Discuss in detail these areas that need accountability and pray together that God will be ever-present in those situations. Check in with each other frequently on this matter as boundaries change constantly with the fluid circumstances of deployment. Ask someone you both trust to join you in prayer over this and, if need be, provide extra accountability and support.

6

BOREDOM

FAITH

Him: "The sluggard craves and gets nothing, but the desires of the diligent are fully satisfied" (Prov. 13:4 NIV 1984).

Her: "A little sleep, a little slumber, a little folding of the hands to rest—and poverty will come on you like a thief and scarcity like an armed man" (Prov. 6:10–11).

HOPE

David came home after twelve hours of stressful work in an air traffic control tower. A 1950s husband would have found his housewife in an apron with dinner waiting. What my husband found was me perched on a stool in my kitchen, staring at an easel across the room. After dumping his stuff on the barren dining room table, he sidled up next to me and matched my gaze.

"What are we doing?"

"Watching paint dry."

Pathetic, I know. The problem with boredom is that it's often a springboard into a much bigger issue . . . laziness. One looks around and says, "I have nothing to do, so I'll just do nothing." Now for those spouses who are scoffing at this topic, whether it's because you have eight kids and haven't seen boredom in twelve years or because you are the deployed member whose day is dictated to you, I challenge you to examine the use of what free time you do have.

Don't misunderstand. There is nothing wrong with relaxing. Psalm 46:10 tells us, "Be still, and know that I am God." Just be sure to nip boredom in the bud before it takes root and robs you of your productivity. Or worse, leaves you feeling as if you have no purpose. Take it on as your mission to find a balance of work and play that gives you an overall sense of well-being.

Sometimes this idea is really hard to bring to fruition in a military lifestyle. We get a deployment behind us and the TDYs start. Then there's the fact that our occupational hazards are rivaled only by ice road truckers or perhaps oil rig workers. So, short of jumping military ship and paddling our lifeboats all the way to the early retirement shore, what are we to do? We must find a balance that maintains our well-being in this crazy life. Let's talk about how to turn your moments of boredom into times when you tend to your well-being.

I give you permission. Start by having a narcissistic moment. What have you done today to enhance your well-being? Maybe we should go back even further. What constitutes well-being? I submit that you can distill it all down to four areas: physical, mental, marital, and spiritual health. The military in general is pretty good at stressing the importance of physical health. And they are getting better at recognizing that mental health is vital to mission success as well. But the health of your marriage and your walk with the Lord largely falls on your shoulders. And the bottom line is those are the two things that will sustain you most in the long run.

Make sure you aren't expending all your efforts on one particular area. None of them can be completely neglected for long. Find a balance. At the end of every day, reflect on what went well and areas that could stand improvement. Pat yourself on the back for the jobs well done, outline a plan to adjust for errors, and press on. The only thing you control in this military life is yourself. Take good care of yourself and use that well-being to care for others. God's will is for you to have a fruit-filled, abundant life in him. And take it from one who knows, unless you're a gifted artist, even something as fun as painting gets boring after a while.

Conversation Starters/Reflection Questions: **Boredom**

1. How much time do you spend on hobbies, watching TV, playing video games, pinning ideas, or scanning social media? Is that too little, too much, or just enough?

2. Do you have any "guilty" pleasures? What are they and why are they considered guilty?

3. What do you find boring?

4. If you had to pick only one way to spend your free time for the rest of your life, what would it be and why?

5. Would you rather exercise your mind, your body, or neither? How often do you do either?

LOVE

Write your spouse a letter describing what you would do together if you had a day with absolutely nothing to do.

DEPLOYMENT

It's very important to keep your boredom from turning into laziness. Go to http://bible-verses-insights.com/2009/06/how-to-stop-being-lazy for ten tips from Bible verses on how to stop being lazy. Try to come up with creative ways to apply these during deployment.

And this week, make it a point to talk to each other about the four aspects of well-being. Discuss improving any areas that need polishing and come up with ways of encouraging one another in the effort.

7

FINANCES

*"A budget is telling your money where to go
instead of wondering where it went."*

—Dave Ramsey, *financial guru*

FAITH

Him: "Wisdom is a shelter as money is a shelter, but the advantage of
knowledge is this: Wisdom preserves those who have it" (Eccles. 7:12).

Her: "For the love of money is a root of all kinds of evil. Some people,
eager for money, have wandered from the faith and pierced themselves
with many griefs" (1 Tim. 6:10).

HOPE

The cashier offered me a sad and all-too-knowing smile as she handed
me my debit card.

"I'm sorry, it was declined."

I tried to feign more surprise than was actually warranted in my
response.

"What? I don't think that can be. Would you mind trying it again?
Sometimes the strip on the back gets so worn that it doesn't read it."

She swiped the card again and simply shook her head before handing it back to me. Completely embarrassed, I watched her push the cart loaded down with bags of groceries off to a corner.

"If you'd like, there's a bank and an ATM in the BX next door. I can suspend the order until you get the money to come back and pay for it. But you'll have to do it soon before they restock the items."

I fought back tears as I left the commissary. My husband was a newly minted Second Lieutenant in the Air Force, and I was a newly minted wife. We had both entered the marriage with tens of thousands of dollars in student loans. And prior to getting his bachelor's degree, my husband had financed an entire associate's degree on a credit card with a 28 percent interest rate! Our debt didn't stop there. I had been the victim of a crafty credit card company that targeted teenagers, and I had brought my own significant amount of consumer debt as a dowry.

After we tithed and all our bills were paid, we always struggled to make ends meet each month. Knowing this, I just started the car and pulled out of the parking lot. Since it was long before the invention of the smartphone, I went home and called my bank. The automated teller told me that we had $207 in our checking account. The grocery bill had been $221.

When my husband came home for dinner that night, he found me crying over the two bowls of cereal I had set out on the table.

"What's the matter?" He wrapped his arm around my shoulders, and I pressed my face into his side. I recounted for him everything that had happened, and over our meal of generic Cheerios, we started one of the most important discussions we would ever have. We decided that night that we needed to have a budget. We needed a plan that would keep us from falling into the quicksand in which so many couples find themselves.

I wish I could say that was the last time my card was ever declined. It wasn't. It was a long, hard road to financial freedom. Eleven years later (yep, it took that long), we decided to join some friends in taking the military edition of Dave Ramsey's *Financial Peace University*. In the weeks of going through the program, we learned about taking baby steps to getting out and staying out of debt. We cut up credit cards and paid off our remaining balances starting from smallest to largest using a method he calls the debt snowball. I will never forget the celebration when we were finally debt-free.

The Bible promises that God will supply all our needs according to his riches (Phil. 4:19). But you can't just sit around and expect the money to manage itself. We are expected to be good stewards of our money. Matthew 25:21 says, "His master replied, 'Well done, good and faithful servant! You have been faithful with a few things; I will put you in charge of many things. Come and share your master's happiness!'"

If we can't be trusted to appropriately manage the resources we are given, why in the world should we expect the Lord to deposit an overwhelming abundance? Be faithful and godly with your finances, no matter how miniscule they may seem. It will be humbling and perhaps embarrassing to eat cereal for a few meals a week in order to put the money you save into paying off a debt. But that embarrassment will pale in comparison to the joy of one day having such an abundance that you feel led to buy the groceries for the embarrassed young girl in front of you at the store when her card is declined.

As Dave Ramsey says, "If you will live like no one else, later you can live like no one else."[2]

Conversation Starters/Reflection Questions: **Finances**

1. In what kind of financial situation did you grow up? Were your parents realistic about living within their means?

2. How important is it to you to be debt-free? Is there such a thing as good debt?

3. Who handles the finances in your marriage? Why? Is that the best situation, or would it be better for you both to have a deeper understanding of your financial situation?

4. Are there any hidden problems with finances or spending habits about which you have not been completely honest with your spouse? Discuss your understanding of what is and isn't appropriate spending.

5. Do you currently have a budget? When was the last time you talked through your budget? Discuss any adjustments that need to be made.

LOVE

Where your treasure is, there your heart will be also. You should treasure and cherish your spouse. Write a letter that declares this to him or her and commit to valuing this person more than any possession, pursuit, or earthly treasure.

DEPLOYMENT

Hopefully, you had more than one discussion about your finances before your spouse deployed. Regardless of whether you think you have your situation handled, you should always keep communication open about your spending, saving, and budgeting.

Numerous resources exist to aid in getting your finances in order. We found it particularly helpful to use a faith-based system that took into account our desire to tithe and continue charitable giving while paying off debt. There are even resources available for extreme financial crisis. This list includes resources I have either used myself or seen used with success by others.

Budget-Driven Resources:

Dave Ramsey

www.daveramsey.com

Crown Financial Ministries

www.crown.org

Urgent Needs:

Military One Source

www.militaryonesource.mil

Air Force Aid Society

www.afas.org

USAA Financial Services

www.usaa.com

Red Cross

www.redcross.org

8

PRODUCTIVITY

> *"The way we measure productivity is flawed.*
> *People checking their BlackBerry over dinner*
> *is not the measure of productivity."*
>
> —Timothy Ferriss, *American entrepreneur*

FAITH

Him: "Work willingly at whatever you do, as though you were working for the Lord rather than for people" (Col. 3:23 NLT).

Her: "All hard work brings a profit, but mere talk leads only to poverty" (Prov. 14:23).

HOPE

She sat in a wheelchair rolled underneath the table in front of me. I had seen her from afar all weekend at the Christian writer's conference. She was clearly handicapped from an illness I'm not smart enough to recognize. Her legs were twisted, confining her to the wheelchair pushed by a dear friend. But despite her affliction, her smile never faltered. It was always cheery and never disingenuous. But the final day was different.

As the conferees were led in worship, I witnessed one of the most beautiful things I had ever seen. As the music swelled during the chorus of a well-known hymn, she pushed herself back from the table and, using only upper-body strength and leverage from the table, maneuvered herself to stand. She couldn't raise her hands because she needed both of them to support her weight. But she tilted her head back to face heaven, and I am almost certain I could see her soul lifted in praise.

The desire of her heart was for Christ alone. We were all there to submit ourselves and our writing to the mercy of editors and agents. I have no idea what kind of work she was submitting, but at that moment she herself was the proffer.

We often get caught up in trying to discern what the world has to offer us, what difference we can make in the world, and how to decide the best avenue for using the gifts and talents that God has given us. But what I learned from watching that woman was that while God does care about the desires of our hearts, we must first submit ourselves wholly to him. Even if our bodies, our skills, our abilities seem incomplete or broken. Only then are we equipped to fulfill the plans he has for us.

Dear friends, chase after God's heart. Fall in love with him again. Ask him with a clean heart to give you the desires that reside there. If something has gotten in the way of that pursuit, banish it. Colossians 1:22–23 says, "But now he has reconciled you by Christ's physical body through death to present you holy in his sight, without blemish and free from accusation—if you continue in your faith, established and firm, and do not move from the hope held out in the gospel." The ESV translation says "stable and steadfast." I love that word . . . steadfast. I long for that word in my life. I long for the Lord to tabernacle over me so that I might be steadfast in my walk with him, unable to depart . . . steady and graceful under pressure. That beautiful woman rising from her wheelchair was steadfast though a mere nudge could have sent her to the floor. "On Christ the solid rock I stand, all other ground is sinking sand, all other ground is sinking sand. . . ."

You yourself, and the ability of your marriage to glorify God despite the hardship of separation, is the true testament to your level of productivity. "But seek first his kingdom and his righteousness, and all these things will be given to you as well" (Matt. 6:33).

Conversation Starters/Reflection Questions: **Productivity**

1. What areas of your life (marriage) are you trying to work by your own strength, instead of the Lord's, to see productivity?

2. By what standard do you think the world measures success?

3. How does one do everything, even things like housework or cleaning a weapon, as if for the Lord?

4. What does it mean to do something for the glory of the Lord?

5. Name three things you have done recently that you can say without a doubt you did purely for the glory of the Lord and with no hope for personal gain?

LOVE

Identify an area of your life that you know you need to dedicate to the Lord in order to increase productivity. Write a letter to your spouse recognizing this and the desire for him or her to join you in praying for God's glory to be accomplished in your pursuit.

DEPLOYMENT

It is so easy during deployment to put things on hold or, on the opposite end of the spectrum, to become a workaholic in order to have much to show for the time apart. But our productivity isn't measured by worldly standards. As a Christian couple, it is more important that you are spurring each other on to glorify the Lord in whatever he has called you to do.

Make a list of goals you each hope to accomplish during the deployment. Discuss each goal individually and together decide if they are realistic and God-glorifying. Make a point of talking regularly about your goals and encouraging each other to meet them.

9

EXPECTATIONS

*"Lower your expectations of earth. This isn't heaven,
so don't expect it to be."*

—Max Lucado, *Christian author and pastor*

FAITH

Him: "But when you ask, you must believe and not doubt, because the one who doubts is like a wave of the sea, blown and tossed by the wind. That person should not expect to receive anything from the Lord" (James 1:6–7).

Her: "In the morning, LORD, you hear my voice; in the morning I lay my requests before you and wait expectantly" (Ps. 5:3).

HOPE

What to Expect When You're Expecting. What to Expect the First Year. What to Expect the Second Year. I had all the books. What I didn't expect when ordering them as a bundle online was how thick each volume would be! And now they've even published *What to Expect Before You're Expecting*! I am not disparaging these books, by any means. They are highly insightful and valuable tools for parenthood. I only mention them as proof that expectation management is clearly a highly useful concept when preparing for and surviving a significant life event . . . whether it is the birth of a child or the deployment of a spouse.

My husband was a huge fan of the concept of expectation management. He had mastered the art of applying it on a daily basis. Not that he thought we should lower the bar in order to avoid disappointment. He just felt if we laid out the probable outcomes prior to entering into a situation, we would be better equipped to handle whatever happened. Perhaps this is why he is remembered by so many as being flexible and able to handle with grace whatever life threw at him. I have to smile when I think of how this played out over the course of our eleven years of marriage.

I can't tell you how many vacations started with a "family meeting" where we gathered among the suitcases and were "briefed" on what to expect. What to expect going through security at the airport, how long we would be in the car for the road trip, even reminders not to expect bathroom breaks once we started hiking. He urged us to plan ahead and prepare for bumps in the road to occur. I loved this about him because I am a most unorganized, spontaneous person. I am more likely to jump into a situation and figure out what I'm doing as I'm doing it. I tend to forget that sometimes plotting the exit strategy should be one of the first steps in the process.

Before I became a full-time writer, I was a birth doula and natural childbirth instructor. I taught the Bradley Method of Husband-Coached Childbirth. Pregnant women and their husbands filled our living room every Monday for the several years that I taught. One night after the students had departed, my husband pointed out something I had never completely realized.

"You know, Heather, all you're really doing is teaching them expectation management." He smiled, but not in a condescending way. His smile always reassured me that all was right with the world. And he was correct. I taught them what changes to expect in their bodies during pregnancy, what to expect in preparation for labor, and most of all, to expect that anything can happen in labor and child-rearing.

The same applies to life in general. Think of it this way . . . if you are walking alone down a dark alley at night and a hand grasps your shoulder, you're likely going to startle and become frightened. Why? Because you didn't expect it. But if you are walking down the hallway of your church on a Sunday morning and a hand grasps your shoulder, you are likely to turn around with a smile on your face, expecting to see a familiar friend.

Having realistic expectations about deployment can go a long way toward avoiding hurt and disappointment. If you communicate with each other about things like when to expect a phone call, what you can discuss over the unsecure Internet connections, how to not get your hopes up about an early return, or how to curb your disappointment when the spouse on the home front isn't able to catch every sought-after phone call, deployment will feel less like the dark alley with hidden "surprises" waiting to overwhelm you. The key is to be realistic.

There might not be volumes of books titled *What to Expect During Deployment*, but it could pretty much be boiled down to one thought: the only constant in the military is change. And as an homage to my wonderful husband, I will conclude this topic the same way he concluded our "pre-departure briefings," with the cliched phrase: "Expect the unexpected." And I would add, when the unexpected comes, expect God to show up.

Conversation Starters/Reflection Questions: **Expectations**

1. Are you more likely to be the "expectation manager" or the "fly by the seat of your pants" type? Explain why and discuss whether this dynamic works in your relationship.

2. What do you think you can realistically expect during this deployment?

3. Describe a time when something took you by surprise and you wish you had been better prepared.

4. Is there anything you are expecting from your spouse of which he or she might be unaware? Explain.

5. How are you likely to respond if you have managed your expectations and planned for the unexpected, and life throws you a curveball?

LOVE

Write a letter to your spouse detailing how he or she exceeds your expectations in your relationship. Include what he or she can expect from you in terms of partnering to navigate the unexpected.

DEPLOYMENT

A good implementation of expectation management is to forecast, as best as possible, scenarios you might encounter during deployment. Talk through the possibilities that each of you may face. Dig into Scripture to find a verse that helps you know what to expect in that situation or how to handle it. Buy a pack of index cards; on one side write the scenario, and on the other side write the Scripture reference.

I did this for my husband before he deployed. I used envelopes and wrote the scenario on the front and the Scripture reference and a personal word of encouragement on the card on the inside. When he was killed and his personal effects returned to me, those cards were among his things. I learned that much of what I had thought only applied to him also applied to me . . .

On the envelope: What to expect when walking through the valley of the shadow of death . . .

On the card: Psalm 23—"I will fear no evil for your rod and your staff comfort me." Even when darkness surrounds you, you are never alone because you carry my love with you.

10

CHILDREN

*"It is easier to build strong children
than to repair broken men."*

—Frederick Douglass, *African American social reformer and author*

FAITH

Him: "Fathers, do not provoke your children to anger by the way you treat them. Rather, bring them up with the discipline and instruction that comes from the Lord" (Eph. 6:4 NLT).

Her: "Train up a child in the way he should go, and when he is old he will not depart from it" (Prov. 22:6 NKJV).

HOPE

I awoke one morning to a toilet that wouldn't flush. My first instinct, even after sixteen months of not having him there to help, was to call David upstairs to fix it. Once I remembered that no one was going to do it for me, I pried off the lid and reattached the part that had come loose. As I washed my hands, I glanced in the mirror and barely recognized the person staring back at me. I felt I had aged ten years since he had left. How could I not when I was expected to be both mom and dad? When

I delivered three children without pain medication, I honestly thought that would be the most physically exhausting and challenging thing I would ever do. Now I know it pales in comparison to raising three children as a single parent. I love my children dearly, but especially during deployment and times of separation, they can push a weary parent to his or her wits' end.

I really wanted to go back to bed. I wanted to allow myself to indulge in the pity party I sometimes felt entitled to. But that morning, the smell of something cooking made me decide I needed to overcome my desire to retreat and see what my early risers had been up to.

When I walked into the kitchen, I was greeted with "Happy Father's Day, Mommy!" Oxymoron aside, the holiday had completely slipped my mind. A slight panic rose in me over what the absence of their dad might do to my little ones. But they were all merely awaiting my reaction.

My ten-year-old is quite a budding chef, as evidenced by the bird's nests (toast with an egg scrambled in the middle). I decided that I had made the right choice in teaching Home Ec as part of our homeschool curriculum that year. They stood beside the breakfast and beamed up at me. In that moment, all the hard work was worth it to all of us. My heart was filled with the bittersweet taste of my children's words of affirmation. I realized that while children are definitely affected by the separation military life brings, they are resilient and possess an innate ability to make the best of tough situations. And, despite the extra responsibility they can place on the parent on the home front, they can also be a great source of joy and companionship.

I praise God for filling in the gaps where I fail as a parent. He promises to be "father to the fatherless" (Ps. 68:5). And I am so grateful for the people he has put in our lives to come alongside us on this journey. The combination is enough that, though at times we may wear the title of single parents, no child is fatherless.

Conversation Starters/Reflection Questions: **Children**

1. What was the most difficult thing you remember facing as a child?

2. What is the most difficult struggle you have faced as a parent? If you aren't a parent, what is your biggest fear about becoming one?

3. How have you seen resiliency in your children in the past?

4. What are some of the biggest challenges children face during deployment?

5. What are some ways you can support your children through deployment, even while you are struggling with the separation yourself?

LOVE

Write a letter to each of your children individually. In the letters, be sure to reassure them that while you are physically separated, you are still loving them and caring for them. For the spouse on the home front, write a letter to your spouse encouraging his or her efforts to parent from afar. You can also write letters to your children . . . they will be treasured keepsakes one day. If you are not parents yet, write a letter to your future son or daughter. Consider making a commitment now to raise him or her up in the way of the Lord and into a relationship filled with love.

DEPLOYMENT

One of the best things we ever did was to have a "pre-deployment night" with our children. Much of their anxiety can be assuaged by helping them know what to expect. We waited until about two weeks before David's departure to tell them—long enough to ask questions and process but not so long that they worried and felt the dread of what was coming. We got a DVD and books on Afghanistan from the library, as well as the *Sesame Street* video explaining deployment. We watched and read them together and then let them ask questions about where daddy was going and why. Together we made a paper chain with a link for each month he would be gone. We counted out one piece of candy for each week he would be gone and put them in a huge jar. Every Sunday before church, they could each have one piece. "When there's none, daddy's work is done!" And finally, David drew on the lids of small mason jars and wrote the children's names on them. Every week, we would count out enough Skittles or M&M's for each day of the week and put them in the jars. They would have one each day to count down the days and see the reminders of daddy in his drawings.

Another great resource is a Daddy Doll (www.daddydolls.com). You send in a picture of your military member, and it is put onto a stuffed doll or pillow. It is also available with a voice recorder. Before he left, my husband recorded a message for each child. They are priceless keepsakes. Check with your FRG or AFRC; sometimes they have vouchers for complimentary dolls.

On the day of departure, I would recommend that your children stay home with a very close friend or family member instead of going to the departure location . . . particularly if your children are small. Having done both, we found this to be the best way for everyone. We bought small gifts and wrapped them for each child. The morning of David's departure, he sat down with them and explained that they couldn't open the gifts until he left. This created a sense of excitement for them and kept them from feeling overwhelmed with sadness. It also gave me time alone with him in the last moments before he left.

For the spouse left at home, don't be in a hurry to rush back to your children. They are enjoying their presents. You will have plenty of time to be with them and process with them. Sit in your car and cry if you need to. Go get a cup of coffee and spend some time in the Word. As much as possible, process through your emotions. There will be a lot of them.

After saying good-bye, you both should take some time to gather your thoughts and pray. You will be better prepared to go home and focus on your children or to tend to the many missions ahead.

If you are reading this and thinking, "I wish I had done all these things before the deployment," it isn't too late. Have the voice boxes shipped to the deployed member to be recorded over there. FaceTime or Skype while the kids make paper chains. Just don't miss out on the opportunity to include your children in the process of the deployment.

11

COMMUNICATION

*"To listen well is as powerful a means of communication
and influence as to talk well."*

—John Marshall, *fourth chief justice of the U.S. Supreme Court*

FAITH

Him: "A gentle answer turns away wrath, but a harsh word stirs up anger" (Prov. 15:1).

Her: "Set a guard over my mouth, Lord; keep watch over the door of my lips" (Ps. 141:3).

HOPE

One day, not long after his commissioning and a short time before we were to be married, I asked David what was on his agenda.

"Well, I've got PT this morning, then I'm going to TMO to hammer out some details about the PCS. While I'm on base, I'll probably stop by clothing and sales at the BX and pick up a new set of BDUs."

The only thing I gathered was that he was going to the base for clothing. Good communication in any relationship can be difficult. Good communication in a military relationship requires the use of a glossary. Sometimes it's like a child competing in a spelling bee. The stumped participant asks, "May I have a definition, please?" Military acronyms aside, the best dictionary for marriage is one another.

For example, I've spent all day engrossed in the labors of love that make me a housewife: carpool, grocery shopping, errands, and lots of other thankless but necessary tasks that don't have much of a visible end result. My husband comes home, looks around the empty kitchen, and opens the fridge, saying, "What's for dinner?" Unbeknownst to me, he skipped lunch, was inundated with problem solving at work, and had a really strenuous PT session. So his question is entirely motivated by his growling stomach. What I hear is, "What have you been doing all day that kept you from having dinner ready?"

We funnel all information through our own life experiences, knowledge base, thought processes, personality type, and most often, current situation. What makes sense to you might be totally lost on your spouse. Don't be afraid to question, without accusing, what your spouse means by his or her words. If we don't become intentional about our communication, choosing words with careful consideration as to how they can be perceived, we run the risk of creating tension where none existed.

There are so many books and schools of thought about how to be good communicators. But I believe the best advice comes from the book of James: "My dear brothers and sisters, take note of this: Everyone should be quick to listen, slow to speak and slow to become angry" (1:19). Even if it requires a Google search afterward, if you both listen carefully and endeavor always to respond with love, good communication will result.

Conversation Starters/Reflection Questions: **Communication**

1. What are two significant things that happened recently? How did they affect you?

2. The lion, beaver, otter, and golden retriever are used to describe four personality types. Which of the following do you think best describes you? Your spouse?[3]
   - Lion: strong, confident, leader, likes to make sure things get done
   - Beaver: detail-oriented, organized, follows instructions, good with projects
   - Otter: very outgoing, enjoys people, humorous, creative
   - Golden Retriever: loyal, sensitive, encouraging

3. Why is it important to understand each other's personality types in order to be good communicators?

4. Do you find it easier to be a good listener or a good speaker? Why?

5. Is there something you struggle to communicate to your spouse? If so, discuss it now and work on ways to speak openly about it in the future.

LOVE

Meaningful conversation is vital to a healthy marriage. Write a letter to your spouse that describes what you've learned from good communication with one another lately.

_____

_____

_____

_____

_____

_____

_____

_____

_____

_____

DEPLOYMENT

Although we have access to an unprecedented number of communication options during deployment, there are still the challenges of lack of time and delayed connections that can frustrate the situation. Make a list of things you want to talk about before a conversation begins. This will help keep you on track if time becomes a factor.

If you find yourselves in conflict and the conversation must end, make a point of agreeing that the issue still needs to be resolved. It is better to revisit the discussion when you both have had time to cool down and reflect. Try not to let the conversation end in anger but in prayer, asking the Lord to help you work through the situation. Always let the last words your spouse hears be affirmations of love.

12

PATRIOTISM

*"The nation which forgets its defenders
will be itself forgotten."*

—Calvin Coolidge, *thirtieth U.S. President*

FAITH

Him: "Greater love has no one than this: to lay down one's life for one's friends" (John 15:13).

Her: "You have heard that it was said, 'Love your neighbor and hate your enemy.' But I tell you, love your enemies and pray for those who persecute you" (Matt. 5:43–44).

HOPE

We were going to be riding in the belly of a metal whale. After days of scrubbed flights, we finally won the "Space Available" travel lottery, and the kids and I boarded the C-17 in the wee hours of the morning. The ops tempo at my husband's unit in Germany kept him gone more than he was home. So during one of his long TDYs, I decided the kids and I would venture back to the States by ourselves. We took our places in the cargo net seats and, thankfully, the three of them slept the first few hours of the ten-hour flight from Ramstein to Dover, Delaware.

A benefit of military flights is the freedom to move around. Rejuvenated by their nap, the kids took off to explore. When I followed them behind a series of crates toward the back of the plane, I was startled to discover a flag-draped coffin. I screamed at my young and unknowing children just before they climbed on. Then I felt a hand lightly touch my arm. The deep creases in his face and the look in his eyes told me the soldier standing by the coffin had seen much.

"Leave them be, ma'am. That kid died so they'd have the freedom to play. He'd be honored to serve them."

That day we were given the honor of being in the presence of true American patriots. What I considered merely a flight to transport cargo and people like us was, in reality, a flight to take a brave soldier home. The flag draping his coffin would eventually be folded and given to a grieving family member. The soldier I met was his escort, seeing him all the way to his final resting place. There are some traditions that have deep meaning, and this is one of them.

Patriotism is less about zeal for the country itself and more about fervently supporting and remembering those willing to die for it. And why else would our citizens be so willing to lay their lives on the sacrificial altar of freedom if not for love of country. We might not always agree with our government's politics. But we should all recognize that the presence of patriotism, like the display I witnessed on the plane, is vitally important to the sustainment of the privileges we have in our great nation.

Conversation Starters/Reflection Questions: **Patriotism**

1. What do you feel is the greatest freedom we experience here in America?

2. As Christians, how do you reconcile the duties of a profession of arms?

3. Is it possible to take a life in defense of your country and still believe in the sanctity of life? Explain.

4. How have our country's views of patriotism changed in the last fifty years?

5. How is it possible to love our enemies as Jesus commanded and still be patriotic?

LOVE

Deployed member: Write a letter to your spouse explaining why you are willing to lay your life on the line in defense of your country.

Spouse: Write a letter to your spouse supporting his or her decision to voluntarily take up a profession of arms.

_____

_____

_____

_____

_____

_____

_____

_____

_____

_____

_____

DEPLOYMENT

Buy an American flag for the deployed member to carry during deployment. If possible, display it in the background for the family members at home to see during video teleconferencing, and bring it along on missions. Upon return, proudly display or fly the flag at your home. It will have a new, personal meaning.

13

DEATH

*"Life is not measured by the number of breaths you take,
but by the moments that take your breath away."*

—Original author unknown

FAITH

Him: "Even though I walk through the valley of the shadow of death, I will fear no evil, for you are with me" (Ps. 23:4 NIV 1984).

Her: "For I am convinced that neither death nor life, neither angels nor demons, neither the present nor the future, nor any powers, neither height nor depth, nor anything else in all creation, will be able to separate us from the love of God that is in Christ Jesus our Lord" (Rom. 8:38–39).

HOPE

When the bus carrying soldiers pulls away from the curb, every spouse left behind wills it to turn around for fear that it will be the last sight of their loved one. Every soldier on patrol wonders if death will be their new companion. If you've given your heart to the Lord, you are spiritually ready for death from the moment of acceptance on. But nothing truly prepares someone for the news that a loved one has died. Nothing truly prepares someone to stare their own death in the face. So instead of trying to prepare for how to handle death, learn to take nothing in this life for granted.

Rest in the assurance that the Lord watches over his people. Psalm 116:15 says, "Precious in the sight of the LORD is the death of his faithful servants." Does that mean he relishes our destruction? No. It means not one hair on our head is disturbed without him knowing. It means that no dusty, hidden alley in Afghanistan that poses threat after threat is unknown to the Lord who created the universe. If he cares enough to track our every move, how much more is he moved by our passing from this world to eternal fellowship with him? We should therefore have no fear of death—because nothing can separate us from him. Let us not fear what is to come. But in the meantime, let it motivate us to cherish the moments experienced together.

One of my favorite authors is Mitch Albom. In his book *The Five People You Meet in Heaven*, a man named Eddie dies. The following excerpt is said to him by someone he meets in heaven:

> "Lost love is still love, Eddie. It takes a different form, that's all. You can't see their smile or bring them food or tousle their hair or move them around a dance floor. But when those senses weaken, another heightens. Memory. Memory becomes your partner. You nurture it. You hold it. You dance with it. Life has to end," she said. "Love doesn't."[4]

Alfred, Lord Tennyson said, "It is better to have loved and lost than never to have loved at all." I disagree. I don't think love can ever be lost. True love—the kind that defies logic, that drives out fear, that brings peace by its presence alone . . . agape love—is too powerful to be lost.

True love tattoos itself on your heart. You are scarred. In a good way. It's a scar that serves to remind you of something so powerful it transformed the landscape of everything it touched. Like fire consumes everything in its path—nothing is more complete in its devastation. This love becomes woven in the very fiber of your being. You can no more accept its absence than you can deny you are you.

The manifestations of that love will never return when someone you love is taken from you. You can no longer breathe in their essence, hear their laughter or their whispered *I love you* in your ear. Their touch leaves your skin, and you will eventually forget the exact creases of the hands that you loved so much. Hands that held enough strength to crush you but held you gently instead. When those precious things are gone and your beloved can no longer hold you physically . . . the greatest of all remains. It is their love that will hold you forevermore. Because true love can never be lost. True love is transferred from their being to yours, and you carry it with you until you are reunited in the presence of the One who is Love.

Take comfort in the knowledge that while death at some point is inevitable, the thought of it doesn't need to consume you. Dwelling on the "what ifs" only robs you of the joy life has to offer now. And most important, should death rear its head in an untimely manner, the Lord promises to walk with you and comfort you through the valley. Nothing can separate you from his love. There is life after death. Live in a way that when you die, others will know your Savior lives.

Conversation Starters/Reflection Questions: **Death**

1. Have you ever had a "close call"? Describe it.

2. Which part of death scares you most? What can you do to remove that fear?

3. If you knew today was going to be your last, what would you do?

4. What has been your favorite part of life?

5. If you were to die tonight, do you know beyond a shadow of a doubt that you would go to heaven? (If the answer to this question is no, I urge you to seek out a chaplain or pastor and learn more about the life-giving freedom that comes from a relationship with Jesus.)

LOVE

This might be the hardest letter you will ever write. But I promise you that if something does happen to you, it will be the most precious to your spouse. Write the letter that you would write if you knew these words were the last your spouse would ever read from you. Hold nothing back. Say the things you struggle to say in life. Say the things you know will comfort their heart. Hold their heart with your words. (Though it's tempting, do not open the letter from your spouse unless they are his or her last words.)

DEPLOYMENT

Having a conversation about death before or during a deployment can be very difficult. But it is better to deal with death when it is a possibility versus a reality. You've likely started this conversation already when updating your wills and power of attorney as part of the deployment checklist. So just take it to a personal level and candidly discuss your wishes for your spouse after your death. This applies not only to the deployed member, but also to the spouse on the home front.

I pray none of the things you discuss will need implementing. But some topics to consider are attaining goals or fulfilling dreams you've made together, caring for loved ones, even remarriage. Removing your spouse's questions of how you would feel about his or her future decisions will leave them with one of the biggest gifts you can give . . . peace of mind.

14

WORRY

"Pray, and let God worry."

—MARTIN LUTHER, *father of the Protestant reformation*

FAITH

Him: "Therefore I tell you, do not worry about your life, what you will eat or drink; or about your body, what you will wear. Is not life more than food, and the body more than clothes? . . . Can any one of you by worrying add a single hour to your life?" (Matt. 6:25, 27).

Her: "Give all your worries and cares to God, for he cares about you" (1 Pet. 5:7 NLT).

HOPE

A wildfire was burning in Waldo Canyon, Colorado. For the first two days, aside from the occasional comment about smoke plumes rising behind the front range, it garnered little attention in the area I lived. Then, while loading groceries in my van on what would become an infamous Tuesday, I glanced up at the mountains and saw the fire crest the ridge. Strong winds from an afternoon thunderstorm met it on the other side. The fire exploded down the hills and into the urban areas at the base of the mountain. What ensued sent me to the book of Revelation. The scene was nothing short of apocalyptic. The sun was blotted out by an eerie orange smoke that clogged our lungs and stung our eyes. It rained ash and burning embers on all of Colorado Springs. Even the newscasters cried as a stunned population watched the fire devour homes, communities, and landmarks. I honestly don't know of any natural disaster more thorough in its devastation than fire. It consumes everything it touches.

My husband was in Afghanistan. So my three children and I watched from our house about six miles from the devastation as the fiery monster began its death march toward the city. Thirty-two thousand people scrambled to get out of its path. I began to pack the family albums, collect important documents, and throw clothes into suitcases just in the event we would be the next ordered to evacuate. Despite the fact that we lived on the side of town farthest from the fire, I worried instead of prayed. I was so focused on the mess that I almost failed to see the Messiah in a time when we needed him most.

Worrying about the circumstances surrounding us is like saying God isn't big enough to handle the situation. When I finally saw worry for the waste of energy it is, I decided to do something more productive. We prayed for the firefighters that valiantly held the fire at bay. We took in refugees . . . at one point there were seven people (one a pregnant woman), a dog, and a turtle in our house. We prayed with them through the waiting to learn the fate of their homes. In the end, hundreds of people lost everything, and tens of thousands of acres were destroyed. It was a reminder to us all that the things of this world are fleeting and can change in an instant, but the Lord remains the same. And I learned the Lord and his mighty angels can protect us and our concerns far better than my worry can.

Conversation Starters/Reflection Questions: **Worry**

1. Does God bring natural disasters as punishment? Explain.

2. About what do you tend to worry most?

3. How does one go about giving all cares to the Lord?

4. Do you believe in destiny? If so, how does this influence your tendency to worry?

5. How do you distinguish between contemplative preparation and worry?

LOVE

Using an example of a previous time your spouse successfully overcame the temptation to worry, encourage your spouse to cast his or her cares upon the Lord now.

DEPLOYMENT

What are some things couples worry about during deployment? Discuss them openly with each other. Be sure to validate your spouse's concern, but work together so that neither of you becomes an alarmist.

 86

15

CRISIS

"When written in Chinese, the word crisis is composed of two characters—one represents danger, and the other represents opportunity."

—John F. Kennedy, *thirty-fifth U.S. President*

FAITH

Him: "Consider it pure joy, my brothers and sisters, whenever you face trials of many kinds, because you know that the testing of your faith produces perseverance" (James 1:2–3).

Her: "Shall we indeed accept good from God and not accept adversity?" (Job 2:10 NASB).

HOPE

"There's been an accident." These words strike fear in the heart of even the most steadfast individuals. When the news comes via telephone call in the early morning hours, it can be downright crippling. In 2005, my husband was training for CCT selection and was spending countless hours in the pool for water confidence training. This exercise was normally not a problem for my husband, as he was in excellent physical condition. But unbeknownst to him on this particular morning, he was fighting an upper respiratory infection.

The procedure for underwaters, as they're called, is to swim a lap, quickly reoxygenate, and swim the other lap. Assuming he had properly gained enough oxygen to sustain him, David proceeded to the other end of the pool. According to the lifeguard on duty, when she saw him floating facedown, she assumed he had transitioned to the drown-proofing portion of his routine. Six minutes later, she finally pulled his lifeless body from the water. David's buddy had also been at the pool and called me with the news as he followed the ambulance to the hospital.

The doctors at the small local hospital did all they could for him. But his level of trauma was above their capabilities, and he was transported via helicopter to a higher level trauma center. Against protocol, the flight paramedics allowed me to come along because they honestly didn't expect him to survive the fifty-minute flight. Taking only my purse and the Bible David had left in the car, I prayed and filled myself with God's Word as we lifted off. Earlier in the week, I had finished reading *The Hiding Place* by Corrie ten Boom. In horrendous conditions at Ravensbruck concentration camp, she was prompted by the Lord to give thanks in all circumstances. As I watched the medics work frantically on my husband's lifeless body, I wondered how Corrie, constantly surrounded by death, found it in her to have peace and hope. I knew I served the same God she had and so I beseeched him for the grace he had extended to her.

In a feeble effort to be useful, I leaned to open a trash bag for one of the medics and lost my place in the Bible. It fell open to a page in the back where my husband had written Philippians 4:4–5, "Rejoice in the Lord always. I will say it again: Rejoice! Let your gentleness be evident to all. The Lord is near." I decided to make that my covenant with the Lord. I would commit to being gentle and calm in the midst of this crisis, regardless of the outcome, if he would allow me to know that he was near. But to rejoice in those conditions felt impossible. Then I remembered something else Corrie alluded to in her book. You don't have to be thankful *for* all circumstances. There are some things that you just can't be happy about. But you can choose to be thankful *in* all circumstances. I looked around. All that came to mind at that moment was that I was thankful my husband wasn't dead yet. I clung to that.

We landed and they whisked David away. The rest of the day went by in a fog, but I kept my promise to the Lord and stayed calm during the storm. My husband was put on life support in the Serious Intensive Care Unit, and we were advised to call in the family. That night we held a prayer vigil and begged God for a miracle. I had shared verses with those around me throughout the day, but I kept the verse in Philippians to myself. During the vigil, David's squadron commander, a wonderful Christian man who had been by my side since arriving at the trauma center, pulled me aside.

"Heather, there's a verse that has been coming to mind today as I've watched you navigate this ordeal." You guessed it . . . he quoted Philippians 4 to me. I'm crying as I write this just like I did then. At that moment, I knew the Lord was indeed near, and a peace I honestly can't explain came over me. Three days later, my husband defied all odds and, to the amazement of the doctors, awoke from his coma completely unscathed. He was given a clean bill of health and had no recollection of any of it. But I carry enough remembrance for us both. And I learned we don't need enough faith to move a mountain until we are faced with a mountain that needs moving. Faith the size of a mustard seed is sufficient. God will provide the rest.

Conversation Starters/Reflection Questions: **Crisis**

1. To whom are you most likely to turn in a crisis? Why?

2. If faced with a crisis situation, how do you feel you would respond? Are you or your spouse more likely to be calm and collected?

3. Have you ever been in grave danger? What got you through it?

4. Do you believe that God causes bad things to happen?

5. Is it possible to triumph in tragedy? Explain.

LOVE

Write a letter describing a time when you faced a crisis but still experienced joy and triumph. Your spouse will love the reminder of your strength in adversity.

DEPLOYMENT

I wish I had better news. A crisis is going to happen during your deployment. It never fails—the car will break, the fridge will go out, a child will break an arm, a mission will go awry, or the air conditioning in your hooch will quit running. It is up to you to make the best of it. For the deployed member, begin to prepare yourself mentally for how you will allow God's peace to be a key component in your response to a crisis. For the spouse at home, make a list of resources from which to pull in the event something does occur. And most importantly, make the Lord your first call.

16

THANKFULNESS

*"Thanksgiving with the mouth
stirs up thankfulness in the heart."*

—Dr. John Piper, *Baptist preacher and author*

FAITH

Him: "But I will sacrifice to You with the voice of thanksgiving. That which I have vowed I will pay. Salvation is from the Lord" (Jonah 2:9 nasb).

Her: "Give thanks in all circumstances; for this is God's will for you in Christ Jesus" (1 Thess. 5:18).

HOPE

It was the day before Thanksgiving, the first major holiday since my husband had been killed. I realized I needed a few last-minute items from the store so I could assemble my contribution to the meal we were to share with some friends the next day. The kids and I threw on flip-flops and jumped in the car. As I sat waiting for the light to change so I could turn, a man in uniform across the street caught my eye. He was tying a Christmas tree to the top of his vehicle. His excited children were jumping up and down as they watched. When he was finished, he turned and embraced his wife, and the happy little family loaded themselves into the car.

The person in the vehicle behind me honked his horn repeatedly, and I wiped the tears from my eyes so I could see to drive. I pulled into the grocery store parking lot but couldn't bring myself to take the keys out of the ignition. I searched my heart for some reason to be grateful. I tried. Really I did. But honestly, at that moment, I found nothing but the kids in the backseat.

I backed out of the parking space and decided we would go for a drive to clear my head. At first I thought I would make the twenty-minute drive to the commissary and complete the task I had set out to do. But there was a long line at the gate to the base, so I just kept driving. The kids fell asleep, so I kept driving for the next three hours. They woke up a bit confused. But when my daughter read the signs out loud and discovered we were in New Mexico, they realized this was more than a trip to the grocery store. It had turned into one of mom's spontaneous road trips. By this point, my children had come to expect the unexpected from me and just go along for the ride. I have a Jeep Wrangler, and driving it is very therapeutic. On more than one occa-sion, my solution to grief has been to load everyone in, roll the windows down, turn the music up, and drive until I can breathe again, stopping only for gas. That day turned out to be no different.

We ate dinner at a Taco Bell in some random small town hundreds of miles from home. My concerned friends called, and I regretfully informed them that I wouldn't be running in the 5K I was signed up for the following morning, and we wouldn't be able to make it to lunch the next day. I felt bad that my friend had worked hard planning the meal. But not making it to the grocery store was the least of the reasons I could no longer contribute. We loaded back in the Jeep, and I decided to head toward home. I drove through the night and managed to make it to within an hour of Colorado Springs before I had to call it quits. I herded my sleepwalking children into beds in the Holiday Inn and was asleep nearly before my head hit the pillow.

Thanksgiving Day dawned to us in a motel, clothes from two days prior, and lots of grumbling. My kids were whining about everything. And I couldn't really blame them after what I had put them through. But the thing that frustrated me the most was that I felt the same way in my own heart. We ate breakfast in the lobby and I opened the newspaper as we sat there. The story I read was of a soup kitchen serving a Thanksgiving feast to the local homeless in a downtown train station. I loaded the kids again and headed downtown. We managed to find a parking space and get in line. Quite honestly, we didn't look out of place considering the disheveled clothes and unbrushed hair from our travels. The kids' questions led me to a great dissertation on thankfulness and a reminder that not everyone has the blessings we take for granted.

The doors opened for everyone to be allowed in, and from nowhere a man approached us.

"Oh, you're in the wrong line," he said. "Those here to serve don't need to wait in line. Just come with me and I'll get you set up."

"But we aren't . . ." I didn't get my sentence out before he had taken us by the arms and was moving us through the large crowd. He dressed us in aprons and plastic gloves and pointed us toward the serving line. I looked down at my kids who were taking it all in stride. So I picked up the spoon to dish out mashed potatoes. My kids offered rolls to each person who came through.

We had been there for a couple of hours when I felt someone tap me on the shoulder. A man stood holding a large camera on his shoulder, and a reporter asked if he could interview me and the kids. Seriously? I couldn't help but think it was only in God's sense of humor that he would put my nervous breakdown-induced adventure on the six o'clock news.

We rolled into my friend's house around dinnertime that day. When they asked what we had been up to, I just got the remote and turned on the TV.

My oldest daughter's sound bite summed it up. "My dad was killed in Afghanistan in August, and my mom told us we were going to the grocery store yesterday, but we ended up spending the night in a hotel, and now we're here. I really have seen I have SO much to be thankful for at home still."

Sometimes we have to be stripped of things we hold dear in order to understand thankfulness. It is easy to get so caught up in what we've lost, what we don't have, or what we hope to acquire that we lose sight of the grateful heart God designed us to have. You are surrounded by blessings. They are there regardless of your circumstances because they are born when you choose to say, "I am thankful."

Conversation Starters/Reflection Questions: **Thankfulness**

1. For what are you most thankful?

2. What is the difference between giving thanks *in* all circumstances versus *for* all circumstances?

3. Do you struggle to see your blessings when life is difficult? What can you do to transform your heart so that you may have a more grateful nature?

4. Describe a time in your life when you chose to be grateful for what you have, and God blessed you even more.

5. List five blessings currently in your life of which you know you aren't deserving. Focus on those things this week.

LOVE

Write a letter to your spouse describing all the things about him or her for which you are thankful. Thank your spouse for the things he or she does for you that make you grateful to have chosen him or her as your partner for life.

DEPLOYMENT

I completely understand that deployment gives many circumstances for which it is a struggle to be grateful. But you are capable of having a heart full of thanksgiving regardless. Don't overlook the everyday blessings that exist despite the geographic location of your spouse and the hardships that ensue from the separation.

In your journal, make it a point to write down everything you are grateful for as it comes to your mind throughout the day. Be intentional about counting your blessings. Some days there may be only one or two entries, and they may seem insignificant. Today I was grateful for a Jeep Wrangler when I awoke to two inches of snow and school wasn't cancelled. Today I was blessed by the fact my MRE was not scrambled eggs. Learn to cultivate a spirit of thanksgiving even when there doesn't seem to be anything for which you can be thankful. You will find you are so much more blessed than you realized.

17

FULFILLMENT

*"It is not in the pursuit of happiness that we find fulfillment,
it is in the happiness of pursuit."*

—Denis Waitley, *American writer*

FAITH

Him: "Such a person feeds on ashes; a deluded heart misleads him"
(Isa. 44:20).

Her: "Why spend money on what is not bread, and your labor on what
does not satisfy?" (Isa. 55:2).

HOPE

Have you ever felt a gnawing in your stomach that inhibits you from
accomplishing anything until it's satisfied? So you eat and eat but can't
understand why you never feel full—until you realize you weren't
hungry at all. What you really needed was a drink of water. In life, it's
just as easy to mistake one need for another. But true fulfillment only
comes from the Lord and the pursuit of his will. Even the Israelites,
God's chosen people, struggled with this. They went so far as to fashion

idols to worship because, despite everything God promised and provided, they failed to realize it was only the Lord who satisfies completely.

Now I doubt any of you reading this have statues of golden cows on your mantel, but in reality we aren't that far removed from it. The human tendency is to want something tangible in which to put our faith. It's easier to understand and have confidence in things we can see, things we've earned. We might not physically bow down in worship to our idols, but the way we fill our time becomes idol worship. Our modern world says money is what makes it go 'round, so we feel more secure when we have it. We think if we can just get the latest gadget, more influential friends, or a job that has our spouse home more often, then we will be content. We get so caught up in the pursuit of such things that we fail to notice they have become idols. Beth Moore says, in a sense, an idol is anything we try to put in a place where God belongs. God created a void inside each of us in order to draw us back to him.

So what happens if we don't abandon our idols? What happens if we continue to delude ourselves into thinking that our fulfillment can be bought, earned, or attained in any way other than through a relationship with Christ? Let's dig a little deeper into this week's memory verse. "Such a person feeds on ashes; a deluded heart misleads him. . . ." There lies the sad outcome of such idol worship. Instead of feasting on the Lord's provision, we learn to settle for ashes. A heart that is deluded will mislead the entire person. Matthew 6:21 says, "For where your treasure is, there your heart will be also." If your heart treasures most the things that will fade and cannot satisfy, it is deluded, and you are destined to be misled if you follow it.

When family life is upset by deployment, it is even more tempting to create idols because a part of what makes us whole is absent. But idols are a cheap substitute for the living God. Instead of filling your life with the pursuit of happiness, find joy in pursuing the Lord and allow him to fulfill you.

Conversation Starters/Reflection Questions: **Fulfillment**

1. What do you find most fulfilling?

2. Are you easily drawn into a "keeping up with the Joneses" mentality? Why?

3. What things present in your life could easily take the shape of an idol?

4. What's something you enjoyed doing as a child but haven't done in years?

5. Explain what you think it means to find joy in the Lord. Is this easier or more challenging to do during deployment?

LOVE

Write a letter to your spouse thanking him or her for the fulfillment he or she brings to your life.

DEPLOYMENT

Pray out loud together that the Lord would reveal to you the areas in your lives that are cheap substitutes for him and the things he has planned. Continually remind each other that even though you are apart, the Lord and your family are all you need to be fulfilled.

18

FAITH

*"A little faith will bring your soul to heaven,
but a lot of faith will bring heaven to your soul."*

—DWIGHT L. MOODY, *American evangelist & publisher*

FAITH

Him: "Truly I tell you, if you have faith as small as a mustard seed, you can say to this mountain, 'Move from here to there,' and it will move. Nothing will be impossible for you" (Matt. 17:20).

Her: "Now faith is confidence in what we hope for and assurance about what we do not see" (Heb. 11:1).

HOPE

A little over a year after David died, I was really struggling with which direction I was supposed to go next. I met my husband when I was nineteen years old. We were married a year and a half later, and for the next eleven years the Air Force pretty much dictated my life. We had very little say in where we lived, when we moved, how much he made, or even what his work hours would be. I quickly learned the easiest thing to do was embrace this. I started to be grateful that it took the pressure off me to make most of the big decisions. The flip side to that, however, is that I never really learned what it is like to rely on complete faith in the Lord for confidence in making decisions. Provisions, for the most part, felt like they were provided by the military.

So at thirty-three years old and a single mom of three kids, I found myself staring out my window one day and incredibly frightened at the realization that I had no clue what to do with my future. As I was looking out, one of the few birds that had not flown south for the winter caught my attention. It perched confidently on the branch of a tree that was barren of everything but tiny red berries. It pecked at these little jewels, and as it did I was reminded of this verse: "Look at the birds of the air; they do not sow or reap or store away in barns, and yet your heavenly Father feeds them. Are you not much more valuable than they?" (Matt. 6:26).

I was reminded that God has promised to provide everything we need to thrive in this life. But something we often lack is faith. We struggle to ask with expectancy. We should have faith that he will do what he says he will do. Childlike faith. It was kind of embarrassing to admit that, in some ways, even that bird had more faith than I did. I have no idea how he knows which of God's provisions are intended for his consumption. But he lands on that branch knowing he will be sustained.

I think we get so wrapped up in trying to plan and provide for ourselves—or as often happens in my case, to depend so heavily on others to do it for us—that we forget we are called to put our trust completely in the Lord for provision. Since David's death, many people have said, "Oh, I just don't know how you do it. I just don't think I could do it." I always try to tell them first, don't give me the glory for anything. Any strength I have comes from the Lord. But also, we don't need faith the size of a mountain to get through our everyday lives.

God is bigger than the mountain in front of you. We are told that we only need faith the size of a mustard seed to say in the name of Jesus, "Move, mountain!" James 1:6 NASB says, "But he must ask in faith without any doubting, for the one who doubts is like the surf of the sea, driven and tossed by the wind."

We can all learn something about faith from that bird on my tree. There is no need to worry about where our provision, our direction, our fulfillment will come from. It is by faith you are saved. It is the first of the three things that will remain (faith, hope, and love) when all else fades away. Have faith in faith.

Land where you are and ask in faith for God to provide. My prayer is that every day we might be like that little bird and consume the proffers of a Savior who is all we need to take flight.

Conversation Starters/Reflections Questions: **Faith**

1. What is the difference between faith, trust, and belief?

2. In what areas of life do you struggle the most with placing complete faith in God to provide?

3. Why do you think you have such a difficult time trusting God in that area and not so much in others?

4. Do you believe that miracles still happen? If yes, give an example of one you've witnessed.

5. Why is faith in God to do what he says he will do, and be who he says he is, so important?

LOVE

Write a letter to your spouse encouraging him or her to place complete faith in the Lord to provide for all needs.

_____

_____

_____

_____

_____

_____

_____

_____

_____

_____

_____

_____

_____

_____

_____

_____

_____

_____

_____

_____

_____

DEPLOYMENT

Deployment absolutely places strain on everyday life. Without each other's physical presence to lean on, your faith in the Lord to provide for all your needs is crucial to thriving during this time. Make a list of needs—being sure to include personal, spiritual, financial, and so on— that you feel will need to be met during deployment. Pray together over each need and commit them to the Lord in faith that he will provide.

19

FEAR

"Courage is fear that has said its prayers."

—DOROTHY BERNARD, *silent screen actress*

FAITH

Him: "Though an army besiege me, my heart will not fear; though war break out against me, even then I will be confident" (Ps. 27:3).

Her: "For God has not given us a spirit of fear, but of power and of love and of a sound mind" (2 Tim. 1:7 NKJV).

HOPE

I had been asked to speak at a retreat for Haitian missionaries. Denise was part of a team from Idaho that had come to serve those who were taking a brief break from full-time ministry. She and her group led us all in worship, watched the kids, and brought the Word of God for our encouragement. But this woman had to overcome more than anyone to be there. She had aerophobia, a crippling fear of flying.

I watched her shed tears of terror and clench the hands of her friends as they practically carried her to the small plane leaving Port au Prince for the Dominican Republic. They tell me it was the same when she flew commercially to Haiti on her very first flight ever. She has grandchildren she has never met because her fear has kept her away. But she felt so strongly about heeding God's call to serve in the Dominican Republic that she cast aside her fear to follow him. That is courage. That is complete and utter dependence on the Lord to sustain her.

First John 4:18 says, "There is no fear in love. But perfect love drives out fear, because fear has to do with punishment. The one who fears is not made perfect in love."

She loved God so much that she made a conscious decision, a decisive action that helped her turn to God and away from sin. For her, and for many, fear was sin. Courage to face that fear was the prescription for breaking the chains that bound her.

"It is for freedom that Christ has set us free. Stand firm, then, and do not let yourselves be burdened *again* by a yoke of slavery" (Gal. 5:1; emphasis mine). Again. That means it's normal that we fall over and over. It is when we find courage and make the decision to do a 180-degree turn from our struggles that we break the cycle. It is the moment we choose to allow God to rein in every area of life. The moment when we decide that the love of Christ, who has already paid the penalty for our sin through his work on the cross, is worth more than anything else. Only in him can the chains that bind us really be broken and the Spirit of the Lord abound.

Deployment presents so many opportunities for fear to seize your willing spirit and immobilize you. But it is up to you to pry fear's icy fingers from your heart and find the courage to face this time in your life. He is able to give you courage to walk into enemy territory with the confidence that he goes before you and is your rear guard. He can give you courage to face the challenges on the home front that wear you down and make you extra vulnerable to sin. Today, in this moment, decide once and for all to trust the Lord to sustain you . . . it is your own decisive action to accept God's free gift of liberty that will bring courage. Because if God is for you, who can be against you?

I wish I could say that once we learn to be like the David of the Bible, slaying the Goliaths in our lives, it is smooth sailing from there on. But in fact the Bible, and even David's own story, promises the exact opposite. In John 16:33, Jesus tells his disciples, "I have told you these things, so that in me you may have peace. In this world you will have trouble. But take heart! I have overcome the world." God doesn't intend for us to live in a constant state (or spirit) of fear. He wants us to exchange those fears for trust in his will for us and then receive a peace that only he can give. Fear in a life governed by deployment is inevitable. But fear itself isn't the problem. It's what we do with it that makes all the difference. Let the fear that holds the power to cripple be a motivator to press into the One who made the lame walk and the fearful fly.

Conversation Starters/Reflection Questions: **Fear**

1. As a child, were you fearful of anything or anyone? If so, how did you overcome it and how long did it take?

2. What is a current personal fear you would like to banish?

3. Is being fearful a sin? Why or why not?

4. What do you think is the biggest fear for most people? Why?

5. What advice can you give your spouse on how to conquer fear when you aren't able to weather a storm together?

LOVE

Write a letter to your spouse that reassures him or her of God's protection and sovereignty.

DEPLOYMENT

Courage is the antithesis of fear, so spend your energy this week reiterating your admiration for each other's bravery in less-than-ideal circumstances. If you identify potential sources of fear, you can better anticipate them and therefore not be overcome by them. Share with one another what you are afraid of. Sometimes just vocalizing your fears goes a long way in alleviating them.

20

PEACE

*"A crust eaten in peace is better than a
banquet partaken in anxiety."*

—AESOP, *ancient Greek author*

FAITH

Him: "And the peace of God, which transcends all understanding, will
guard your hearts and your minds in Christ Jesus" (Phil. 4:7).

Her: "Now may the Lord of peace himself give you peace at all times and
in every way. The Lord be with all of you" (2 Thess. 3:16).

HOPE

Ask pretty much anyone, particularly those in the military, to give a
definition of peace, and they will most likely relate it to the absence of
conflict. But the peace of the Bible is nearly antithetical to that idea.

Jesus told his disciples, as it reads in John 14:27, "Peace I leave with
you; my peace I give you. I do not give to you as the world gives. Do not
let your hearts be troubled and do not be afraid." If peace meant the
removal of conflict, opposition, separation from loved ones, or anything
else that disrupted a copacetic existence, then would their hearts have

run the risk of being troubled or afraid? Not according to conventional wisdom. The average definition of peace would have had Jesus say, "Here's world peace. You'll never face hardship again."

But, much to the chagrin of his disciples, I'm sure, he didn't say anything close to that. He actually promised the opposite. "I have told you these things, so that in me you may have peace. In this world you will have trouble. But take heart! I have overcome the world" (John 16:33). There's the key . . . *in me.*

Jesus knew the hardship that lay ahead for his followers. He knew that if men persecuted him they would also persecute those who came after him and sought to follow his teachings. But he assured them that they would not be alone. That he was leaving them with the Holy Spirit. An evidence of a true believer is fruit of the Spirit. And one of the greatest gifts of the Great Comforter is peace. Not just in the still and quiet moments or the cease-fire and treaty signings. That isn't the peace I'm referring to. It is in being able to look at the chaos surrounding you—the death, the destruction, the horrible things this world throws at us—and in the midst of that say it is well with my soul. It is a peace that surpasses all understanding. A peace that defies logic.

For me, peace comes in recognizing the ways that God reveals his presence in the toughest of life's situations. And, moreover, being reconciled to the fact that God might not plan on alleviating any of the pain. Knowing he is with me when everything falls apart allows me to take a deep breath and feel at peace.

We learn and grow the most through the trials in life. Years down the road, people aren't likely to remember what trial you faced. What they will remember is the way you faced it . . . bringing glory to God through grace that can only come from God's peace. So take heart: greater is He who is in [us] than he who is in the world (1 John 4:4 NASB). Remember, peace is not something you attain. Peace is something you receive. So come to the Lord with empty palms open toward him and accept it.

Conversation Starters/Reflection Questions: **Peace**

1. What does it mean for something to transcend all understanding? Can you experience something, embrace it, or invite it, if you can't comprehend it?

2. Some common phrases are "make peace," "be at peace with," and so on. How do these thoughts differ from peace, the fruit of the Spirit, to which the Bible refers?

3. Is there an area of your life or marriage where peace, meaning the ability to walk through the struggles with a steady heart, seems impossible? Explain.

4. Describe a situation where your heart should have been troubled, or everything around you seemed to be out of control, but you experienced a peace that surpassed all understanding.

5. Is "world peace" a realistic goal or even possible? Why or why not?

LOVE

Write a letter to your spouse that will "speak peace" into his or her weary heart in the midst of the chaos he or she is bound to face during your time of separation.

_____

_____

_____

_____

_____

_____

_____

_____

_____

_____

_____

_____

DEPLOYMENT

Even though it is different from the peace referred to in other sections of this topic, it is important to "make peace" with certain things you will likely see, do, think, and feel during deployment. Talking openly about what makes your heart troubled or fearful will help in that process. For security purposes, the downrange spouse may not be able to discuss everything and that's okay. But be sure to encourage one another to try to let the peace of God guard your hearts and minds during this difficult time.

21

HUMILITY

"Humility is not thinking less of yourself,
it's thinking of yourself less."

—C. S. Lewis, *author and Christian apologist*

FAITH

Him: "And what does the LORD require of you? To act justly and to love mercy and to walk humbly with your God" (Mic. 6:8).

Her: "When pride comes, then comes disgrace, but with humility comes wisdom" (Prov. 11:2).

HOPE

I could hear the cries of my nine-month-old daughter wafting through the air vents. She was wailing at the top of her lungs in protest over being left in the nursery downstairs. I tried to focus on the discussion in the women's Bible study I was attending at our church in Germany. My husband had been deployed for six weeks with at least three more to go before his return. My youngest of three was attached at my hip, and it had been quite a battle to separate her for my much-needed break. I took a deep breath and tried once again to tune out the sound. I looked around to see if anyone else seemed to notice. Kids are always louder to their parents than they are to others, I reassured myself. At least that's what my friend had told me as she convinced me to give the Bible study a try.

Her invitation to the study came on the heels of a very trying phase in my life. We had moved to Ramstein, Germany, when my youngest daughter was just six weeks old. Our household goods had not even arrived before my husband's ops tempo was in full swing and sent him on what would become one of many assignments that kept him gone 285 days that first year. The combination of postpartum depression, single parenting three kids under age four, and the challenges of living off base in a foreign country, resulted in a less-than-pleasant me.

My sweet friend graciously took on the role of confidante and counselor, babysitter, and all-around go-to gal for me. Many an afternoon I could be found sleeping on her couch while she took a turn pacing the floor with my colicky infant. As soon as life threatened, I picked up the phone where her number was on speed dial. After several months of this routine, the Lord began to remind me that he should be my first stop. My first reaction when trouble comes should be to pick up my Bible, not the phone. And not only that, but he started to remind me that even the Son of Man came to earth to serve and not to be served (Mark 10:45). During this time, I had a tendency to think only of myself. I would disregard everything and everyone else in order to get my needs met. I was soon to learn that this was a recipe for a lesson in humility.

I finally caved and slipped quietly from the room to rescue my baby from her apparent torture. The nursery workers assured me that she was fine and her crying didn't bother anyone but me. Despite all this, and the stated policy of no children in the study, I quieted her down and slipped back into the room upstairs. I rationalized that all the women in that room were moms and would understand how badly I needed the "break," even if it included holding a squirming infant.

When the study was over that evening, my friend gave me a sideways hug, shot me a sad smile, and shrugged as if to say, "Well, we tried," and then headed out. I gathered all my stuff and buckled Ava into the infant carrier. Of course, by then she was sound asleep. I was almost out the door when I felt a tap on my shoulder. The facilitator of the Bible study wore a patient but frustrated look.

I assumed she was going to console me for having to endure a colicky baby and a hectic life and thank me for coming. So I prepared myself to be a martyr and jumped right into the role with false modesty.

"I hope I didn't disrupt the class too much. I'm sure you understand what it's like to have a fussy baby and an absent husband."

"Yes, I do. But that's actually what I was coming to talk to you about. Unfortunately, I'm going to have to ask you to either not bring your baby into the study again or please refrain from coming back."

I could feel the flush of embarrassment paint my cheeks. I opened my mouth to defend myself, but she wasn't finished delivering my lesson in humility yet.

"Every one of these women has been in your shoes . . . some of them currently. But we are intentional with our request for no children present in order to give all of you a much-needed break and change of scenery."

Something inside of me flipped, and the words that came out of my mouth were less than humble.

"Well, if we aren't welcome here, we just won't come back."

I stormed out the door, snatched my other two kids, and burst into tears as I buckled everyone into the car. I couldn't get my phone out fast enough to call my friend and tell her what had happened. As I was dialing the number, my four-year-old daughter decided to tell me what she had learned that night in her class. She handed me a strip of paper that was cut into the shape of lips with these words: "Set a guard over the door of my mouth, O Lord."

I remembered the prompting from the Lord lately about going first to him before my friend. I decided to shut my mouth and my phone and pray as I drove home that night. I cried myself to sleep but managed to fight the urge to vent everything to my friend. The next morning she called me.

"What in the world happened last night?"

"Why do you ask?"

"I got an email. I think it was a mistake that I was cc'd on it, but it was from the woman in charge of Bible study to the other facilitator. She explained everything that happened with you and was asking her to pray for the situation and advise her on how to handle it."

Tears were streaming down my face, but oddly they weren't all sad tears. I had obeyed and gone first to the Lord. But in a strange twist that only he could have orchestrated, my friend found out without my telling her, and I was given the gift of her godly counsel anyway! We prayed through everything and decided that I needed to apologize and give the study another try . . . the right way.

Humility comes from facing hardships that force us to realize our need for a savior in order to overcome. We are called to live humbly, thinking of others before ourselves, regardless. Sometimes in that submission we find that things happen to us that are downright painful and aren't our fault. Like Job, we are humbled by merely existing in the circumstances of life. Other times we are brought to our knees in humility by the sin of willful disobedience. Either way, we will eventually be humbled. The important thing to remember is that it is a valuable part of living the Christian life. And ultimately, all things work together for the good of those who love the Lord and are called according to his purpose (Rom. 8:28).

Conversation Starters/Reflection Questions: **Humility**

1. What is the difference between humility and being humiliated?

2. Why do you think the Bible says that the meek shall inherit the earth (Matt. 5:5)?

3. Describe a situation in which you have been humbled. What did you learn from that lesson in humility?

4. Other than when using oxygen masks on an airplane, and the instructions clearly state that you should save yourself before assisting others, is there ever a time when you should put your needs before someone else's? If so, explain.

5. How hard is it to be humble in your closest relationships? Why do you think that is?

LOVE

Write a letter to your spouse describing the reasons he or she is worth considering more highly than yourself. Reaffirm your commitment to place his or her needs above your own.

DEPLOYMENT

It is reality that during deployment each spouse must to an extent learn to be self-sufficient and look out for himself or herself. But it is also an almost imperceptible shift to becoming self-righteous and feeling like the world owes you something because of the hardships the military lifestyle brings. And during a time of separation, it is easy for couples to forget the importance of keeping each other's needs at the forefront of their minds.

Set aside a specific time in your routine to be intentional about checking in on your spouse's needs. If you each live for the other first, you will both be the most important person in someone's life, and your needs will be met.

22

COMPLAINING

*"The one who complains about the way the ball bounces
is likely to be the one who dropped it."*

—Lou Holtz, *American football coach*

FAITH

Him: "Do not grumble against one another, brothers, so that you may
not be judged; behold, the Judge is standing at the door" (James 5:9 ESV).

Her: "Do everything without complaining and arguing, so that no one
can criticize you. Live clean, innocent lives as children of God, shining
like bright lights" (Phil. 2:14–15a NLT).

HOPE

"You want to do what?" I sat on the couch feeding our youngest of three
children and stared at my husband in disbelief.

"I want to go back into TACP."

The Tactical Air Control Party was the career field my husband had
been in while enlisted. But at the time of his commissioning, the Air
Liaison Officer title (the officer equivalent of TACP) was only for rated
officers. But he explained to me then, only thirteen months after we had

moved to Germany, that they were opening up a new 13L career field, and if he was selected, we would be moving within six months. It would mean that he had to go back through the TACP schoolhouse at Hurlburt Field in Florida. He would be living in a dorm for the entire time.

The idea made my head spin. TACP was in the special operations community. That meant it would be a difficult process to get in, not to mention adapting to that lifestyle. I knew it would mean hardship for our family. I knew it would mean sacrifice on my part.

My first reaction was to complain. So I did. Pretty much through the entire process leading up to our move. I whined about the amount of hours he spent in physical preparation. I whined about the hassle of PCSing overseas so soon after getting to Europe. I complained about the separation we would be facing on a daily basis for nine months. I finally even started complaining to the Lord. My "quiet time" began to be consumed with my whining instead of being still and listening. Soon, my life was filled with nothing but the sound of my own grumbling.

When we arrived in Florida and got settled into our new home, my husband finally sat down with me and, in the firm gentleness I loved so much about him, told me how it really was.

"Heather, I love you. I don't want you to be unhappy. But this is my dream job in the Air Force. It would mean a lot to me if you would get on board. I don't want you to not share your feelings. But could you please try to be a little more positive? It makes me feel like you aren't supportive of me when you complain all the time. That's not who God created you to be."

Wow. Talk about a wake-up call. My husband was one of the most nonconfrontational people I knew. For him to say something to me about my whining meant it had reached epic proportions. I decided then that I would not complain the entire time we were in Florida. I took it on as a challenge to find a positive spin on everything.

First Thessalonians 5:18 says to give thanks in all circumstances. Not *for* all circumstances . . . but *in* all circumstances. I decided that, instead of complaining about everything, I would give everything to the Lord and ask him to help me find a way to be thankful in all circumstances. Instead of being upset that my husband had to sleep in a dorm instead of with me, I went to bed every night thanking God that I knew where David was and that I knew he was safe. Instead of envying the time he got to spend conditioning his body for the physical demands, I thanked God for an incredibly healthy and good-looking husband.

The transformation in my heart was a gradual one. But it was profound. My outlook on life changed. My husband felt loved and supported and therefore felt freed to speak my love language in return.

Cessation of complaining isn't just about making life more comfortable for those around you. Negativity in your life will drain you of joy. Replace it with life-giving truth, and you will see complaining for the waste of time and energy it really is.

Conversation Starters/Reflection Questions: **Complaining**

1. About what are you most likely to complain and why?

2. Describe a time when being around a negative person has affected you.

3. Describe a time when your whining has produced a negative reaction instead of the sympathy and positive change for which you were hoping.

4. Do you think there is ever an appropriate time to complain? Explain.

5. Why do you think the Bible commands us to do everything without complaining or grumbling?

LOVE

Write a letter to your spouse apologizing for the times when you have been less than supportive with your words. Encourage him or her in a new way.

_____

_____

_____

_____

_____

_____

_____

_____

_____

_____

_____

_____

_____

_____

DEPLOYMENT

During few times in your marriage will you be presented with more fodder for complaints than during deployment. But never is it more important for spouses to feel loved and supported than during the difficult time of separation. Make a list of your five biggest complaints about your current situation. Talk through them and come up with ways to persevere through them and replace the negativity with positive encouragement.

23

DISAPPOINTMENT

"We must accept finite disappointment,
but never lose infinite hope."

—Martin Luther King Jr., *civil rights activist*

FAITH

Him: "In their hearts humans plan their course, but the Lord establishes their steps" (Prov. 16:9).

Her: "And we know that in all things God works for the good of those who love him, who have been called according to his purpose" (Rom. 8:28).

HOPE

It's easy to become frustrated and confused by pseudo-motivational catchphrases, such as, "Every cloud has a silver lining," or "Don't sweat the small stuff...and it's all small stuff." All things we face in life present an opportunity for disappointment. Perhaps they are small in the grand scheme of things, but to the one experiencing it, they certainly don't feel insignificant. And what is one to do when the only clouds visible are those of a gathering storm?

Christian writer Jack Zavada says, "When our prayers aren't answered as we desired and our dreams become shattered, disappointment is a natural result." He goes on to say, "After many years of hurts and frustrations, I finally realized that the question I should ask God isn't 'Why, Lord?' but rather, 'What now, Lord?' God can take our disappointments and work them for our good. When that happens, we come to the staggering conclusion that the all-powerful God of the universe is on our side."[5]

To say there will be disappointments during deployment is an understatement. They run the gamut from the temporary disappointment of a missed phone call to a deeper disappointment that follows missed first steps or a high school graduation. We also have a tendency to hinge our hopes and daily fulfillment on the same things we did when our family unit was intact. And then when things don't turn out like we anticipated, we are left feeling disappointed and bitter. But that doesn't have to be the end result. Disappointment, while it never feels insignificant at the time, is for the most part temporary. Typically there will be another opportunity . . . maybe not for the exact same thing, but another opportunity nonetheless. But most importantly, God promises to work all things for the good of those who love him. While we might not be able to see the silver lining, we can always trust the One who created the clouds.

Conversation Starters/Reflection Questions: **Disappointment**

1. Does disappointment typically bring you down or does it motivate you to try harder? Why do you think that is?

2. What has been the biggest disappointment in your life?

3. How is being disappointed different from being a disappointment?

4. If the Lord determines your steps, as Proverbs 16:9 says, why bother making your own plans?

5. Describe a world where everyone accomplished everything they set out to do and disappointment didn't exist.

LOVE

Write a letter to your spouse reassuring him or her that, while you are disappointed you can't experience life's ups and downs together, you will do your best to keep each other connected and not get discouraged.

DEPLOYMENT

This activity is fantastic if it can be done prior to deployment. But if not, it can still be done via Skype, FaceTime, or phone conversation. Sit down together with calendars for both of you and discuss the events that will be missed during the entire duration of the deployment. Make sure to note things like piano recitals, first swim meets, and easily overlooked yet significant details—not just birthdays and anniversaries. This will help eliminate the disappointment that comes from feeling "forgotten" on a special occasion.

A tradition my family loves is to have a celebration day before my husband deploys. We get a big cake and decorate it for every holiday, birthday, and special event that he will miss. Anyone who has a birthday while he's gone gets their picture made individually with daddy, and we sing to each person. On his or her actual birthday, we watch the video and remind ourselves that a celebration of life is still a celebration regardless of the day it takes place.

24

BITTERNESS

"It is a simple but sometimes forgotten truth that the greatest enemy to present joy and high hopes is the cultivation of retrospective bitterness."

—Robert Menzies, *Australian statesman*

FAITH

Him: "Get rid of all bitterness, rage and anger, brawling and slander, along with every form of malice" (Eph. 4:31).

Her: "Let us then approach God's throne of grace with confidence, so that we may receive mercy and find grace to help us in our time of need" (Heb. 4:16).

HOPE

Halfway through writing this book, my husband was killed in Afghanistan. I'm not going to lie—I questioned everything I knew about God. I wondered why I bothered to pray if the prayers for David's safety, offered by so many, were unanswered. In the three weeks that followed his death, I found myself encouraging others but unable to console myself. A friend called this the "widow's grace." People would approach me for a hug, and I would find myself comforting them instead. I had hidden God's Word in my heart, and when needed, it didn't return void . . . at least when I spoke it to others at the seven ceremonies we had to honor and remember my husband in the weeks immediately following his death.

But I can only explain that display as muscle memory, similar to the way my husband used to prepare before a jump. The motions of opening a parachute are rehearsed over and over again. The repetition ingrains the procedure into the very fiber of the jumper's being. So when the time comes to deploy the chute, the body responds correctly regardless of emotions or circumstances that come from the free fall.

As I sat down to work on this chapter, it was the first time I had written since the morning of David's death. I jumped into a free fall when I opened the door for the notification team. So a month later, when I sat down to write, I grappled with the Lord still. It was the first day I could approach the throne of God without resentment. I should rephrase that. It was the first day I entered into an honest conversation with him about my resentment. When I finally did, he allowed me to leave my bitterness there with him. He took me to Habakkuk 3:19 where I was reminded that though everything seems desolate and barren, the sovereign Lord is my strength, and he will take me over this mountain.

Deployment presents many opportunities for bitterness. Its occupational hazard offers even more. But if we allow ourselves to harbor resentment, it is like saying we don't believe God was or is in control of the situation, and our plan is better than his. Proverbs 16:9 NLT tells us, "We can make our plans, but the LORD determines our steps." The last time I checked, we weren't equipped to play the role of God. It's okay to be disappointed when things don't go as planned. But we mustn't dwell there. We must focus instead on what remains lovely and pure. It matters less that it is muscle memory that deploys the chute, and more that a life is saved when it does.

Conversation Starters/Reflection Questions: **Bitterness**

1. What's the difference between bitterness and resentment?

2. What issues are possible sources of bitterness during deployment?

3. Have you ever felt betrayed by God?

4. What do you think happens if bitterness isn't addressed?

5. What do you normally do to let go of bitterness or resentment?

LOVE

Write a letter to God. Ask him any questions you may have. Petition for help in determining the root of any bitterness you may be holding on to. Read your letters to each other.

DEPLOYMENT

What "mountain" are you facing during this deployment? If you are resenting your spouse or the military for something, confess it to each other and to the Lord and pray together for the Lord to help you see ways of overcoming it.

25

HONESTY

"The real things haven't changed. It is still best to be honest and truthful; to make the most of what we have; to be happy with simple pleasures; and have courage when things go wrong."

—Laura Ingalls Wilder, *author of the Little House on the Prairie series*

FAITH

Him: "The LORD detests lying lips, but he delights in people who are trustworthy" (Prov. 12:22).

Her: "Whoever would love life and see good days must keep their tongue from evil and their lips from deceitful speech" (1 Pet. 3:10).

HOPE

I remember once sneaking into the kitchen and gorging myself on Creamsicles . . . you know, the orange and white push pops on a stick. It wasn't long until I regretted my decision. My mom didn't even need to punish me. The hours I spent kneeling in the bathroom, sick to my stomach, were the consequences. To this day, I can't stand even the smell of orange cream anything. Even as children we are innately sinful. As adults, our poor choices unfortunately come with bigger price tags.

But being honest isn't just about avoiding consequences . . . although consequences can be great motivators for change of behavior. The bigger picture is that of truth. Speaking truth, living in truth, discerning truth from lies. Thinking that sin can forever remain secret is one of the worst lies we can tell ourselves. Proverbs 9:17 NRSV says, "Stolen water is sweet, and bread eaten in secret is pleasant."

The problem with bread eaten in the dark is that we can't see the mold. Satan has a way of taking a legitimate need and a legitimate solution and sliding it almost imperceptibly into a gray area, or sometimes into darkness altogether. The result is ultimately catastrophic. We begin to rationalize sin. We engage in behaviors that are not true to the character Christ created us to have. We take advantage of those God has placed in our lives and cause our brothers and sisters to stumble.

I myself have seen the ramifications of allowing sin to become comfortable. I have felt the consequences of making excuses for wrong decisions. I have experienced the pain and suffering that came when I used God's grace as a license to sin (Jude 1:4). I selfishly wanted so badly to feel good, alleviate suffering, and keep up appearances that I was willing to look the other way and pretend I didn't know the cost. This infidelity cost me precious friends. My actions damaged relationships. The landscape of my life was transformed by my actions.

I confess I am chief among sinners. I have been a Pharisee. In Matthew 23, Jesus admonishes the Pharisees, but notice the hope of redemption buried in the middle of this passage, at verse 26.

> Woe to you, teachers of the law and Pharisees, you hypocrites! You clean the outside of the cup and dish, but inside they are full of greed and self-indulgence. Blind Pharisee! First clean the inside of the cup and dish, and then the outside also will be clean. . . . You are like whitewashed tombs, which look beautiful on the outside but on the inside are full of the bones of the dead and everything unclean.

In the same way, on the outside you appear to people as righteous but on the inside you are full of hypocrisy and wickedness. (25-28)

Dear friends, we should pray that the hidden sin in our lives would no longer taste sweet, but bitter. That it would not only be bitter when we consume it, but also that it would sour our stomachs so we no longer have a taste for the things that are detestable to God. What do you do when you chow down on a grape that turns out to be sour? You spit it out and reach for a drink of water to get the taste out of your mouth.

Why do we continually hunger and thirst for that which won't satisfy? Christ is the living water, the only one capable of cleansing the palate and completely satisfying seemingly insatiable desires. Stop settling for lies instead of truth. Jesus said, "I am the way, the truth, and the life." Hunger and thirst for him. We are all sinners and fall short of the glory of God. But we don't have to believe the lie Satan tells us about being irretrievable from our fallen state. Rid yourself of deception and walk in the freedom of truth.

Conversation Starters/Reflection Questions: **Honesty**

1. Describe an experience where you were less than truthful and felt the consequences of your actions.

2. Describe a time when you were faced with a decision and chose to tell the truth. Do you think honesty always comes without hardship? Why or why not?

3. Why do you think we as Christians allow sin in our lives and tend to hide it when we know that it is detestable to God?

4. Can you honestly say right now that you are being truthful and true to your God-created character, in every area of your life? If yes, where are some areas that you could foresee a chance to falter? If no, how can you remedy that?

5. Is honesty always the best policy? Why or why not? What do you think of the term "brutally honest"?

LOVE

Feeling confident about your worth is a key component in having the strength to walk in truth. Write a letter to your spouse detailing what you absolutely know to be true about him or her—his character, her good qualities, and so on. Reassure him or her of your receptiveness to honesty with you and about you.

DEPLOYMENT

Honesty with each other during deployment is so important. Examine your current situations, and openly and without judgment discuss with each other the areas that are temptations for secrecy. An element that goes hand in hand with honesty is accountability. Hold each other accountable by asking regularly about these areas. Be careful not to come across as condescending. We are all fallible humans. But be sure also that you are not enabling sin or causing your brother to stumble. You are husband and wife, yes, but before that you are brother and sister in Christ. Take the accountability to walk in truth even further if you need to, and enlist the help of someone in your community, church, battalion, or squadron to serve as an accountability partner.

26

TRUST

*"All I have seen teaches me to trust the Creator
for all I have not seen."*

—Ralph Waldo Emerson, *American poet*

FAITH

Him: "Trust in the Lord with all your heart and lean not on your own understanding; in all your ways submit to him, and he will make your paths straight" (Prov. 3:5–6).

Her: "Trust in the Lord forever, for the Lord, the Lord himself, is the Rock eternal" (Isa. 26:4).

HOPE

As I read the Bible, it's important for me to try to picture the characters as the real people they were. It is easy, for example, to put Jesus' disciples up on a pedestal—above reproach. But they too were human beings. Peter was impulsive, Thomas doubted, and I'm certain they all, like us, struggled with worry, fear, trust, and all the other things that remind us of our constant need for utter dependence on God.

One of my favorite stories is in the book of Matthew. Jesus and his disciples are on a boat, and Jesus goes belowdecks for a nap. Suddenly, a great storm appears and sends waves lapping over the boat. The disciples run in panic. The creator of the universe and master of the waves is literally on the boat with them. Yet still they fail to trust that his presence alone is enough to sustain them. He rebukes them by saying, "You of little faith, why are you so afraid?" (Matt. 8:26). Their typical human response was to immediately beg God to calm the storm. The loving Savior gave them the desired outcome. But how much greater a reward if they had chosen to trust him through the storm.

Deployment is possibly one of the greatest storms your marriage is likely to face. Without trust, in both God and each other, you will likely drown. Once you place your trust in the Lord for salvation, however, you can rely on him for provisions to survive whatever life hurls at you. If both spouses have placed their trust in the Lord, they can also trust each other because of the love that exists between them.

Sometimes we do things that make us untrustworthy. But 1 Corinthians 13:7 NASB says that love "bears all things, believes all things, hopes all things, endures all things." The Greek word for believes is *pisteuo*, which means to trust. When you love someone, you will always believe *in* them . . . even when you may have reason not to believe them or believe that they can provide solutions or comfort. Trust comes from believing in someone.

Sometimes the storms of life inevitably send you running. But if you are both running to the Lord, you'll always know where to find one another because you'll meet in the throne room of his presence.

Conversation Starters/Reflection Questions: **Trust**

1. How important is trust in your everyday relationships? Why should it be?

2. Were your parents too trusting of you during childhood? Were you the type to easily break someone's trust?

3. How do you know for certain you've placed your trust in the Lord?

4. Describe what it means to be trustworthy.

5. In what areas do you struggle to completely trust your spouse?

LOVE

Write a letter to your spouse that includes a vow to be trustworthy and to place your trust in the Lord for sustainment throughout the deployment.

_____

_____

_____

_____

_____

_____

_____

_____

_____

_____

_____

_____

_____

_____

DEPLOYMENT

If you have identified areas of your marriage in which you struggle to fully trust yourself or your spouse, develop a plan of action for remedying the situation. Any area of distrust that exists before deployment will only be exacerbated during a time of separation. Hold each other accountable and commit these areas, from the beginning, to the Lord.

27

TEMPTATION

"The truth of the matter is that you always know the right thing to do. The hard part is doing it."

—General Norman Schwarzkopf, *United States Army, retired*

FAITH

Him: "No temptation has overtaken you but such as is common to man; and God is faithful, who will not allow you to be tempted beyond what you are able, but with the temptation will provide the way of escape also, so that you will be able to endure it" (1 Cor. 10:13 NASB).

Her: "Keep watching and praying that you may not enter into temptation; the spirit is willing, but the flesh is weak" (Matt. 26:41 NASB).

HOPE

A while back, the catchphrase "What Would Jesus Do?" swept through the Christian community. The WWJD logo was emblazoned on everything from bumper stickers and backpacks to Bibles and bracelets worn by people of all ages and status levels. The hype eventually waned, leaving only remnants of the fad. But the message of that famous question will forever be applicable to our daily lives and decision-making processes. To answer it, however, requires knowledge of the character of Christ and how he behaved.

After Jesus was baptized, he went out into the desert where he was tempted by Satan for forty days and nights. The account in Matthew 4 shows us that Satan appealed to every aspect of Jesus' humanity. He began by addressing the two most vulnerable areas of man: physical need and pride. Jesus had been fasting and therefore hungered. By turning the stones into bread as Satan suggested, he could not only have met his physical need but also flexed his God-sized muscles in response to the taunting "*if* you are the Son of God" comment. But Jesus' weapon of choice was the "sword of the Spirit, which is the word of God" (Eph. 6:17). He resisted the temptation by quoting Scripture.

Any good game player understands a key ingredient to victory is knowing your opponent. The defense Jesus put up became the method Satan used for his next assault. He quoted Scripture in an attempt to rationalize the temptation. How often do we also manipulate the truth to assuage guilt that comes with succumbing to sin? But Jesus deflected that attack as well as the next, by speaking God's Word. At the sound of the Lord's name, Satan had no choice but to flee.

Jesus went to the cross blameless and without sin. The Bible refers to the encounter with Satan in the desert as *tempting*, so feeling the tug of temptation is not in itself sinful. It is what happens next that matters most. This is not, however, an excuse to knowingly place yourself in a compromising position. Paul reminded Timothy in 2 Timothy 2:22 to flee from evil desires.

So when tempted, ask the question, "What Would Jesus Do?" The answer is simple. Speak truth. Hide God's Word in your heart, and when temptation comes, pull from the arsenal you'll have readily available. No temptation—or tempter, for that matter—is greater than he who is in us.

Conversation Starters/ Reflection Questions: **Temptation**

1. Describe a time when you've gotten caught doing something you shouldn't have been doing.

2. How do you feel about the saying, "It's easier to ask for forgiveness than permission"?

3. Why is it important to resist temptation?

4. How would you describe the level of your moral standards?

5. Have you ever been tempted to do something you knew was wrong because you were certain it would never be discovered? Explain.

LOVE

Write a letter to your spouse honestly admitting any temptations with which you struggle. Reflect on what Jesus would do in your circumstances, and offer ways your spouse can help you overcome temptation.

DEPLOYMENT

When separated from your spouse or isolated from anyone to hold you accountable, it is easy to fall prey to temptation. Make it a point to openly discuss with your spouse anything that tempts you to sin. The word *temptation* is probably most often associated with promiscuity, lust, pornography, and other sexual matters. If your issue is with sexual temptation, then by all means address it. But don't consider this topic irrelevant if your temptation is not so blatant. Consider temptations like perfectionism, gluttony, laziness, or pride; they can all be equally damaging if left unattended.

28

PRIDE

"The proud person always wants to do the right thing, the great thing. But because he wants to do it in his own strength, he is fighting not with man, but with God."

—Søren Kierkegaard, *Danish philosopher and religious author*

FAITH

Him: "The end of a matter is better than its beginning, and patience is better than pride" (Eccles. 7:8).

Her: "Love is patient, love is kind. It does not envy, it does not boast, it is not proud" (1 Cor. 13:4).

HOPE

Out of all the topics I've written for this book, this is probably one of the hardest. Pride is a very powerful sin. Some call it the original sin. A sin so common we have even skewed its existence to be something to wear like a badge of honor. But, in reality, pride suffocates the identity that Christ gives and replaces it with a false sense of who we are or who we should be. It enslaves us by convincing us we are owed something, and if we don't have it, it's because we aren't as good as the next person.

Pride convinces us that we should fake it till we make it. And if we can't make it, we should keep our failure to ourselves. It is a double-edged sword that both inflates us to think we can do anything, and then brings us to our knees in shame because we can't deliver. It was my pride that almost kept me from writing about this very struggle. And whenever pride shows up, it usually invites its cousin, fear. But because I felt so strongly that God wishes to expose both for the loathsome things they are, I chose to write about this topic.

My struggle with pride started when I was about seventeen. I looked in the mirror and saw things that weren't reality. But they were my reality. A reality skewed by thoughts that I needed to look like the airbrushed girls on the covers of the magazines I read. That I needed to dress like the celebrities I saw on TV and the popular girls in my high school. I looked at my life and saw a broken home and a desire for approval. Approval came, but mostly because I perfected a façade that hid who I really was and what I was really doing. This reality overshadowed the identity in Christ I should have been developing.

It wasn't long before I started experimenting with things I thought would make me feel better about myself, or, at the very least, numb my reality. Alcohol, promiscuity, and even drugs were my answer to the pain of believing Satan's lies that I would never be as good as everyone else. And when I would stop for a while, my pride was fueled by my ability to do it on my own.

This feeling of control was addictive. It felt good to know I could manipulate my pain by my own hand and thus identify and control an out-of-control situation. An eating disorder developed from this absurd line of thinking. I would go back and forth between bingeing and starvation. By the time I got to college, I had perfected the "art" to the point that even those closest to me had no idea what was going on. It became my answer to stress. When things in life felt out of control, food was something I could control.

When I married David, God used him to help heal the hurt places in my heart and life. I no longer felt so out of control. David provided a sense of stability and security in my previously chaotic life. It seemed that I had conquered my struggle with pride. But that's just it. Pride is deceitful. It comes veiled in an allure that we can do great things in our own power if we just try hard enough. Instead of being honest about my sin and rooting out the pride, I convinced myself that I was fine. I formed a new identity around my husband and his willingness to unknowingly enable my sin struggle to lie dormant.

Then David was killed and my remedy was taken away. I found myself looking in the mirror once again and questioning who I was and whether I was capable of all that I thought was expected of me. There were some victorious moments when God threw me lifelines that provided real and valuable support. But even those I began to take advantage of. As I was forming a ministry to help others and share what God was doing in my life to make beauty from ashes, I was dying inside. The sin struggle with pride had returned. It told me that everyone needed me to be okay. Not only okay, but exemplary. That I once again needed to perfect a façade and that I could rationalize my selfish pursuits. And fear, not wanting to be outdone by pride, whispered in my ear that if I told anyone I was struggling, it would negate the good that was coming from my ministry.

But God is a jealous God. He will not stand by and watch his children be taken captive forever by something his Son died to save us from. A serendipitous accident began to bring things to light. My rationalizations suddenly held no merit. I realized it was time to nail my pride and fear to the cross and confess my struggles. It was not easy . . . quite the contrary, actually. But Hebrews 12:11 says, "No discipline seems pleasant at the time, but painful. Later on, however, it produces a harvest of righteousness and peace for those who have been trained by it." I finally traded pride for peace. But it didn't just happen all at once. Like a splinter takes time to work its way to the surface of the skin and eventually out, pride and its entourage are something with which I must daily go about intentionally waging war. And this will likely be the case until I reach heaven.

Proverbs 16:18 says that pride goes before destruction. It is true. But if you wholly surrender to the Lord, what is destroyed is the pride itself. And what is left is a new creation whose identity is in Christ. I now cling to the promise found in Galatians 2:20: "I have been crucified with Christ and I no longer live, but Christ lives in me. The life I now live in the body, I live by faith in the Son of God, who loved me and gave himself for me."

The life lived totally surrendered to him is far greater than anything our pride-driven selves can engineer.

Conversation Starters/Reflection Questions: **Pride**

1. Read the account of Adam and Eve in the Garden of Eden. How was pride part of their downfall?

2. What is the difference between taking pride in something and being prideful?

3. Why is pride so dangerous?

4. What makes you proud (in a good way)?

5. How does pride stand in the way of a genuine Christian walk?

LOVE

How proud are you of your spouse? Tell him or her in a letter. Be specific.

DEPLOYMENT

You have been asked to defend your country and support those who do. You are likely "proud to be an American." This only becomes sin when you approach it with the attitude that we are better than every other nationality. You likely "take pride in your work and the role you play." This becomes sinful when you begin to think that you are the only one capable of doing your job as well as you do. There is nothing wrong with giving recognition to laudable acts. You are proud of your son when he pulls his grades up or your daughter who finally sticks her landing after months of gymnastics lessons and practice. Pride can be virtuous. During deployment, be sure to recognize the accomplishments in the right context and with humility.

29

FAILURE

*"We failed, but in the good providence of God
apparent failure often proves a blessing."*

—Robert E. Lee, *commander of the Confederate Army*

FAITH

Him: "If the Lord delights in a man's way, he makes his steps firm;
though he stumble, he will not fall, for the Lord upholds him with his
hand" (Ps. 37:23–24 niv 1984).

Her: "For all have sinned and fall short of the glory of God, and all are
justified freely by his grace through the redemption that came by Christ
Jesus" (Rom. 3:23–24).

HOPE

A very dear friend of mine recently gave me a wooden sign she made.
It says, "God is in her. She will not fall." Hoping to be encouraged by its
proclamation, I put it in a place I would see it frequently. But in the days
that followed its placement, I began to question its truth. I'm a broken,
sinful human. How can I not fall? I began to take it a step further and
question whether God was ever in me to begin with since I was pretty

sure that I was falling at that same moment. That thought created a sense of panic in me. We are usually told that failure is not an option. But I'm human . . . what happens if I fail? Epically.

Take another look at the memory verse from Psalm 37. This verse immediately brought to mind the picture of a parent holding the hand of a toddler who is just learning to walk. Hand in hand, you guide her to the destination . . . slowly and carefully. At least you try. I remember one time in particular in my own experience as a parent. I was holding my daughter's hand as we walked along a sidewalk. She wanted so badly to take off running. She was squirming with all her might in an effort for me to release her hand and let her go her own way. When she got excited at her newfound freedom of mobility, she thought she was ready to just take off on her own. But as soon as she tried, she stumbled. A crack in the path we were on brought her unsteady self to her knees. If I hadn't been holding her up with my hand, she would have hit face first. The stumble brought suffering . . . raw places that bled for days until the hurt healed over. But the protection that came from someone wiser than herself, who didn't give her everything she wanted, prevented something much worse from happening.

How like the Father's love. He holds tight to the toddler heart even in its protest and best efforts to explain away the need for guidance. We try to do things our way, even when we find ourselves on the most difficult road ever traveled. But God never lets go. So why would he hold on? If we are given free will, why would he hold so tightly to us when we are determined to go our own way? Because *he loves us*! He loves us too much not to guard what belongs to him. First John 3:1 says, "See what great love the Father has lavished on us, that we should be called children of God! And that is what we are!"

That love is epic. First shown to God's chosen people in the Old Testament, and then through the revelation of Jesus revealed to Gentiles (us) in the New Testament, that love can be applied to all believers. "The LORD appeared to us in the past, saying: 'I have loved you with an everlasting love; I have drawn you with *loving-kindness*. . . . You will be rebuilt, O Virgin Israel. Again you will take up your tambourines and go out to dance with the joyful'" (Jer. 31:3–4 NIV 1984; emphasis mine).

The Hebrew word for loving-kindness in this text is *chesed* or *hesed* (pronounced kheh-sed). A cross-reference is Psalm 103:4; it equates this kind of love with the mercy to redeem one's life from the pit. *Chesed* has become one of my favorite words in the Bible. A love so great that it delves into the pit to redeem the object of its affection! And he called Israel a virgin! After all the times they had defiled themselves and run back to him, only to repeat the whole process, he said, *I will redeem you*. Praise God for redeeming love when we make mistakes.

Matthew Henry's commentary says this of the verses in Jeremiah:

> This is the assurance of the constancy of His love. "I have loved you, not only with an ancient love, but with an everlasting love, a love that shall never fail." Although the comforts of it may be suspended for a time, nothing can separate us from that love! Those whom God loves with this love He will draw into covenant and communion with Himself by the influence of His spirit on their souls.[6]

Jesus promised his followers that he would not leave them as orphans. He said that it was better for him to go than stay (John 16:7). *Better*?! It was better because with his departure came the presence of the Holy Spirit. The Great Comforter. It wasn't a suitable substitute for the living Christ walking in the flesh with those who adored him and left everything to follow him. No, he said it was better! How many times have I wished for the God of Moses, the One who spoke face-to-face and revealed himself with a tangible cloud that led down the path of righteousness? How many times have I said I would give anything to have Jesus with me in person so that I would not allow my own decision-making processes to screw up my life? But Jesus said the spirit that has come to rest on every true believer in Christ is better! I want better!

And in all of this, we gain freedom! Where the Spirit of the Lord is there is freedom. Where there is evidence of the Spirit, there is a child of God. And God delights in eventually giving his children the desires of their hearts when they are aligned with his. I'm so grateful for the literal sign in my life that propelled me to examine all of this. The sign does speak truth after all. Truth: the Lord is in me. And ultimately, in many ways, I will not fall. But I will stumble. I will. It is inevitable. I submit that it's God-created, even. Because it is in the stumbling that we fall in a new way. So here's to falling . . . into and in love with him . . . that we may be upheld by his mighty hand and held in his loving embrace.

Conversation Starters/Reflection Questions: **Failure**

1. Explain the difference between falling and failing. Now explain how you can fail and not be a failure.

2. How accepting are you of others' faults? How quick are you to forgive others' shortcomings?

3. When can failure be viewed as a blessing or a success?

4. Is failure really never an option? Why or why not?

5. Describe a time when you made a mistake and felt like a failure. What did you do to overcome the defeat and move forward?

LOVE

Write a letter to your spouse asking for forgiveness for any unresolved mistakes. Thank him or her for making allowances for your inevitable failures. Affirm your commitment to be forgiving of his or her shortcomings.

DEPLOYMENT

It is hard not to fail each other when functioning in a "normal" family life routine. It becomes even more difficult when separated. The down-range spouse will likely be consumed by tasks at hand and forget things like a child's recital or to ask how the soccer playoff went. The spouse at home is trying hard to be supportive of a mission he or she perhaps doesn't understand or even fully know about. Sometimes this strain causes us to come across as harsh, impatient, or downright mean. Ask yourself if there are areas of your marriage or work situation that could cause you to fail in giving your spouse the support he or she needs. During this deployment, are there mistakes that have been made that need to be forgiven? Talk through these questions together and present them to the Lord for healing and restoration.

30

HOPE

"'Hope' is the thing with feathers—
That perches in the soul—
And sings the tune without the words—
And never stops—at all."

—Emily Dickinson, *American poet*

FAITH

Him: "'For I know the plans I have for you,' declares the Lord, 'plans to prosper you and not to harm you, plans to give you hope and a future'" (Jer. 29:11).

Her: "Be joyful in hope, patient in affliction, faithful in prayer" (Rom. 12:12).

HOPE

"And now these three remain: faith, hope and love" (1 Cor. 13:13a). These three remain. When all else is stripped away, all that matters is that we have faith, hope, and love. They are interwoven. This understanding is so valuable that I think we should spend some time delving into their correlation more deeply.

Let's look at this concept like a chemistry equation, using the cross-reference of Romans 5:1–5 (emphasis mine).

> ¹ Therefore, since we have been justified through *faith*,
> we have peace with God through our Lord Jesus Christ,
> ² through whom we have gained access by *faith* into this
> grace in which we now stand. And we boast in the *hope* of
> the glory of God.

faith ➔ justification through Jesus' grace ➔ glory to God

> ³ Not only so, but we also glory in our sufferings, because we
> know that suffering produces perseverance; ⁴ perseverance,
> character; and character, *hope*. ⁵ And *hope* does not put us
> to shame, because God's *love* has been poured out into our
> hearts through the Holy Spirit, who has been given to us.

Glory to God through suffering ➔ perseverance ➔ character
➔ **hope** = **love**

Faith yields hope and hope equals God's love. "But the greatest of these is love" (1 Cor. 13:13b). The three are interwoven. But hope is the hinge between faith and love.

Hope is the hand that grasps the cliff and refuses to let go. It is what carries you through any difficult situation. Hope gives breath to the widow who stands by her husband's grave with three small children. Hope gives cause to the soldier's act of leaving his family to build a better community half a world away.

Matthew Henry says of Romans 12:12, "God is honored by our hope and trust in him. Especially when we rejoice in that hope. Those who rejoice in hope are likely to be patient in affliction. . . . And prayer is a friend to hope and patience and in it we serve the Lord."[7]

We serve the Lord by being hopeful in the midst of trials. A hopeful heart can withstand any darkness. No one can take away your ability to hope. Hope heals past hurts. It builds bridges to the future. Hope keeps the present dream alive. What do you do when life seems hopeless? You hope against hope. Even if all you can muster is the hope that this too shall pass.

You rejoice. Always. You rest in assurance that your God *will* come. You hope in that. You pray. You cry out. You look to the place you last saw your Savior, and you expect him to show up. Chances are he isn't the one who left. Have faith that hope brings love . . . the greatest of all things.

Conversation Starters/Reflection Questions: **Hope**

1. Are you typically an optimistic person? Why or why not?

2. What things get in the way of having a hopeful outlook?

3. Name three things you hope to see happen in the next year.

4. Can you believe the promise of Jeremiah 29:11 when you look around and everything seems hopeless? Explain.

5. Which is easier for you to relate to—faith, hope, or love? What can you do to strengthen the areas you struggle to embrace?

LOVE

Write a letter to your spouse that gives him or her something to hope for upon the completion of this deployment.

DEPLOYMENT

Sometimes hope is elusive when you are separated from your spouse and family because of a cause you might not fully understand or support. It's hard to remain hopeful that your children, while hurting over the separation, are not necessarily harmed by the process. Maintaining a hopeful outlook can make a big difference in the quality of life for everyone. Try to focus your energies on the hope of a happy reunion.

In the short-term, do things that inspire you . . . take up a new hobby or volunteer. In your journal, start chronicling all the little things that remind you of the Lord's faithfulness as you rejoice in hope despite suffering. Give hope a clear place to reside, and you are more likely to know how to find it when it's needed.

31

SPIRITUALITY

> *"And I will ask the Father, and he will give you another advocate to help you and be with you forever."*
>
> —Jesus Christ, *as quoted in John 14:16*

FAITH

Him: "Even the Spirit of truth, whom the world cannot receive, because it neither sees him nor knows him. You know him, for he dwells with you and will be in you" (John 14:17 ESV).

Her: "And pray in the Spirit on all occasions with all kinds of prayers and requests. With this in mind, be alert and always keep on praying for all the Lord's people" (Eph. 6:18).

HOPE

The last visitor had departed. The funeral home was empty except for my family. My sister squeezed my shoulder and gave me a sad smile, then herded our tired children to the car. I couldn't bring myself to move from David's flag-draped side.

The lights turned off around me except for a single spot over the casket.

"Don't worry. He won't be left in the dark." The aging funeral home director approached me with a rectangular black box in his hands. "I'm going to lock the casket with this key, and it will be yours to keep."

He did as he said and replaced the large silver key before handing the box to me.

"For the one who also held the key to his heart."

I stood there holding the weight of his words in my hands. I had no words of my own. No sense of direction. No clue what I was supposed to do next.

"Take as long as you need to say good-bye. He'll be right here until we bring him to the church for the funeral tomorrow. His escort will be here before the sun even comes up."

I simply nodded in response and he left me and David alone. When he closed the door behind him, I realized that this would probably be the last time my husband and I were ever alone together. My final private good-bye. I wrapped my arms around myself and closed my eyes. My heart ached so badly to just be held one last time in David's embrace. With my eyes still closed, tears came for the first time all day. Hot, liquid emotion streaked my face as I cried out to the Lord in my spirit.

"Why, God? Why did it have to be David? Why did you think I was strong enough to endure this? I just want to feel his arms around me one more time."

Tiny arms slipped around my waist. I jumped and looked down to find Garrett, my son, holding on as tight as he could. At that moment, my sister came running through the door after him.

"I don't know what happened," she said. "He was buckled in his seat, and I was on the other side putting Ava in when he bolted back inside."

My sweet, sweet son looked up at me with glistening eyes. I gave Denise a thumbs up and she left.

"I'm sorry, Mommy. Please don't be mad. I was doing like I was supposed to but then it was like someone told me I needed to come in here and give you a hug."

All the air escaped me, and I knew that God had just answered my prayer. David could no longer hold me because he was in the arms of Jesus. But his son, flesh of his flesh, unknowingly did what his father couldn't do. And he and his sisters were the reason God didn't take me out of my misery.

The words of my Lord flooded my heart. "Rejoice in the Lord always. I am still near."

There is no doubt in my mind that this experience is an example of what Jesus meant when he promised the Great Comforter that would come after him—the Holy Spirit who wishes to abide with believers and show himself in ways we cannot explain.

Mysticism, Kabbala, and all sorts of other new age creations attempt to mimic a state of spirituality that can be very confusing. If you look up the word spirituality on *Wikipedia*, it says it has no definitive definition. So I won't even begin to try to speak definitively on the subject. But I feel strongly that this topic should be addressed because when we are thrust into circumstances such as deployment, our environment can become seemingly unstable and confusing. We have the potential to become vulnerable to new and "enlightened" ways of coping. A desire to stay "grounded" when our world feels upside down can quickly slide into dangerous territory.

Pray that God will give you eyes to see and ears to hear (Prov. 20:12) so that you will not accept anything but the true and living God, manifest in a spirit willing to dwell among believers.

Conversation Starters/Reflection Questions: **Spirituality**

1. Why do you think the world is so fascinated with spirituality?

2. What does "spiritual warfare" entail?

3. Before becoming a Christian, did you ever experiment with other religions? What made you decide that Christianity was the truth?

4. Describe an experience in which you have felt the presence of the Holy Spirit.

5. Does the idea that the Holy Spirit is one-third of the trinity, and yet dwells within you and among you, make you uncomfortable? Why or why not?

LOVE

Jesus recognized that those forced to part with a loved one would need comfort. Write a letter to your spouse with a reminder of the comfort his or her love and relationship brings during this time of separation.

DEPLOYMENT

With so many religions in the world and deployments bringing more and more Christians into direct contact with them, it is more important than ever that we learn what it means to put on the full armor of God. Work through Ephesians 6:10–17 and discuss practical applications of the description there.

32

DISCERNMENT

"Among the gifts of the Spirit, scarcely one is of greater practical usefulness than the gift of discernment."

—A. W. Tozier, *American pastor and author*

FAITH

Him: "But solid food is for the mature, for those who have their powers of discernment trained by constant practice to distinguish good from evil" (Heb. 5:14 ESV).

Her: "And it is my prayer that your love may abound more and more, with knowledge and all discernment, so that you may approve what is excellent, and so be pure and blameless for the day of Christ" (Phil. 1:9–10 ESV).

HOPE

Some days I ask myself, how do I continue to be a slave to sin? Why do I keep returning to that from which Christ saved me? I don't think I can ever lose my salvation. I have the redeeming blood of Jesus over my life and therefore am free from the penalty of death. But we must pray continually for discernment to make wise decisions. We can quench his Spirit in resistance to let go of the ties that bind. And where the Spirit of the Lord is, there is freedom. Freedom comes when moment by moment, breath by breath we choose to rely on the Lord for strength to overcome. But discernment also comes from learning to wait patiently on the Lord for him to direct our decision-making process.

The Bible reminds us that desire without knowledge is not good (Prov. 19:2), and we must constantly place a guard over our mouth. It is when we plow ahead on our own agenda, giving little care to the people around us, that we fall prey to sin. Just because a lightbulb goes on, and it is thought there is a lesson to be shared, that doesn't mean it has to be shared right then. There is value in knowing the appropriate time and place for things. And while maybe God does intend "wisdom" to be shared with others, it doesn't merit an excuse to abandon situational awareness. Sometimes the wisdom comes in having the patience and discretion to feel out the right time.

God's answer or direction to something isn't always yes or no. More than likely it's *wait* . . . then the answer of yes or no will become clear. It is when we take life's timeline into our own hands that we begin to falter. He isn't going to call us to do something that he isn't already equipping us for. If the calling we are hearing is accurate, it isn't going to fade in clarity over time. We are more likely to fail if we jump in prematurely and aren't fully trained or prepared for what he is calling us to. If we wait, seek godly counsel, and submit to the preparation needed to fulfill his purpose for us, then it will be even more effective when put to use.

And remember that everything lasts but for a season. Some seasons last longer than others. But this too shall pass. Before you know it, there will be a new season. A time when there will be no more pain and no more tears. No more heartache from the poor choices we sometimes make.

To me, the following passage from Ecclesiastes reads like beautiful poetry when I am struggling with discerning right from wrong or standing at a crossroads trying to decide which way to go.

> There is a time for everything, and a season for every activity under the heavens:
>> a time to be born and a time to die,
>> a time to plant and a time to uproot,
>> a time to kill and a time to heal,
>> a time to tear down and a time to build,
>> a time to weep and a time to laugh,
>> a time to mourn and a time to dance,
>> a time to scatter stones and a time to gather them,
>> a time to embrace and a time to refrain from embracing,
>> a time to search and a time to give up,
>> a time to keep and a time to throw away,
>> a time to tear and a time to mend,
>> a time to be silent and a time to speak,
>> a time to love and a time to hate,
>> a time for war and a time for peace.
>
> What do workers gain from their toil? I have seen the burden God has laid on the human race. He has made everything beautiful in its time. He has also set eternity in the human heart; yet no one can fathom what God has done from beginning to end. (Eccles. 3:1–11)

In the meantime, we wait. We hold on to the Lord until our knuckles turn white. We pray without ceasing. We hope. In that time between this season and the next we may tilt our head toward heaven and cry out. But even that is for a season. For everything there is a time. In recognizing this, we are free to accept the things we cannot change, break the bondage of sin, and walk in confidence knowing that we are wiser for it.

Conversation Starters/Reflection Questions: **Discernment**

1. How confident are you in your ability to make wise decisions?

2. What circumstances, attitudes, or fears have you allowed to dictate the decisions you make?

3. Describe a time when you felt completely confident you made the right decision when presented with a difficult situation.

4. What does it mean to be a slave to sin? Do you think that a born-again believer can be a slave to sin?

5. What decisive action do you currently need to take to deepen your dependence on the Lord?

LOVE

Write a letter to your spouse describing what makes you confident that one of the best decisions you ever made was to marry him or her.

DEPLOYMENT

Brainstorm together a list of possible decisions that will need to be made during deployment. Go through each item individually and write down possible outcomes so that there is no fear of making a wrong decision when the time comes. Pray together and ask God to banish any worries about your abilities to face your fears and make wise decisions, based on the knowledge that for everything there is a season.

33

NAYSAYERS

"It is a well-known fact that we see the faults in other's works more readily than we do in our own."

—Pablo Picasso, *Spanish painter*

FAITH

Him: "Whatever you do, work at it with all your heart, as working for the Lord, not for human masters" (Col. 3:23).

Her: "Do not let any unwholesome talk come out of your mouths, but only what is helpful for building others up according to their needs, that it may benefit those who listen" (Eph. 4:29).

HOPE

When military members returned home from the Vietnam War, they weren't greeted with ticker tape parades like the previous generation. The overwhelming sentiment of the country was that they had been fighting a lost cause. Many angry citizens even went so far as to spit on soldiers and hurl insults at them. Today, families are faced with egregious acts, such as when the people from a particular Baptist church protest military funerals. The sad fact is that there will always be naysayers. These people habitually spew negativity and create uncomfortable and sometimes painful situations. And it doesn't always take such a blatant display of disrespect for naysayers to have a large impact.

My first experience with the detrimental effects of negativity came when I met Sarah, a newly minted Army wife, thrust into a world about which she knew nothing and could barely tolerate. To add insult to injury, her husband had joined in a rather unanticipated manner and deployed shortly thereafter. We worked through her bitterness until she felt she was ready to let it go. It wasn't until a couple of weeks later, when she once again expressed the same feelings, that I realized the primary problem. The problem was she was buying into the negativity of the people surrounding her.

Dale Carnegie said, "Happiness doesn't depend on any external conditions. It is governed by our mental attitude." People Sarah loved and trusted were fueling her bitterness, most of them unknowingly. It is common for people to speak down on something about which they are ignorant. The military lifestyle, with all its hardships and sacrifices, is a difficult one to understand if you've never lived through it long enough to appreciate some really wonderful benefits.

Once Sarah came to the realization that she couldn't change the feelings of those around her, she focused on strengthening her own Christlike character and committed to a positive outlook. I was amazed at the difference it made not only in her, but also in those in her inner circle. Naysayers have little to say when every venomous arrow bounces off their target and strikes their own heart.

There will be times when we, too, feel tempted to question the mission, the lifestyle, the hardships. It then becomes even more important to remember who we ultimately serve: Christ first, our spouse second. It matters little what others think of our choice to be part of the military extended family. It is Christ alone we should strive to please. If we do everything with the purpose of glorifying him and speak only words of edification to others, we won't need a ticker tape parade. Streets of gold that lead to the Father will be the reward for the decision to follow him, wherever he takes us.

Conversation Starters/Reflection Questions: **Naysayers**

1. How important is it to you that others like you and approve of your decisions? Why?

2. Are you typically an optimist or pessimist? Is there anything that brings out one side over the other?

3. In what ways can you justify your decision to subject your family to the hardships of military life?

4. Have you ever worked or been friends with a habitually negative person? How did you keep his or her attitude from changing yours?

5. Cross-reference Ephesians 4:29. Do your findings change your idea of criticism?

LOVE

Write a letter to your spouse encouraging him or her to stay positive when the situation seems grim or others are bringing him or her down. Find a passage of Scripture to include as encouragement as well.

_____

_____

_____

_____

_____

_____

_____

_____

_____

_____

DEPLOYMENT

During deployment, it is vitally important that, as much as possible, both spouses surround themselves with like-minded, Christian people people. If you don't already have a support network in place, consider getting involved in an organization such as Protestant Women of the Chapel. For the deployed member, it can be more difficult to choose with whom you spend your time. If there isn't a Bible study happening downrange, consider starting one. And always try to make a point of not letting negative people and behaviors influence you. Remember, you ultimately serve Christ.

34

SELF-CONTROL

"To enjoy freedom, we have to control ourselves."

—Virginia Woolf, *English writer and modernist*

FAITH

Him: "Like a city whose walls are broken through is a person who lacks self-control" (Prov. 25:28).

Her: "But the fruit of the Spirit is love, joy, peace, forbearance, kindness, goodness, faithfulness, gentleness and self-control" (Gal. 5:22–23).

HOPE

The story of Esau fascinates me. And, quite frankly, it terrifies me. Hebrews 12:16–17 puts the story of the doomed biblical character in a nutshell: " . . . [Esau] for a single meal sold his inheritance . . . though he sought the blessing with tears, he could not change what he had done." Wow. How like that we tend to be. We give up the blessings that God wishes to give us because we are blinded by what we perceive to be our imminent needs. We rush to make provisions for ourselves instead of waiting patiently on the Lord to provide.

Esau was convinced that he would perish if he didn't have sustenance at that exact moment. He rationalized that the blessings of a birthright would do him no good if he died from starvation (Gen. 25:29–34). He lacked the faith to see beyond his current circumstances. Apparently, like so many of us, Esau had never learned how to be still and trust God.

When we lack self-control, fail to exercise the practice of delayed gratification, and don't completely trust in God to provide for all our needs, we run the risk of forfeiting God's best for us. We become willing to settle for what we can grasp for ourselves instead of submitting to God's plan and will. Now, don't confuse self-control with willpower. Willpower is beneficial when viewed as a motivator to take action, but willpower *alone* negates the need for a Savior and says, "I can do this on my own." Scripture reminds us, "I can do all things *through Christ* who strengthens me" (Phil. 4:13 NKJV; emphasis mine). I think a good way to look at it is that self-control is willpower surrendered to God's will.

If you continue to delve into the story of Esau, you see that later on he used the same means by which he lost his birthright to attempt to gain it back. He thought he could buy back his father's blessing with a meal. He tried to take his future into his own hands. When his plan did not go over well—completely derailed, actually—did he learn from his earlier experience and wait for the Lord to vindicate him? No, once again he lacked self-control.

Before I go any further, I have to say that when I first read this, I felt kind of sorry for Esau. He was after all the victim of a conspiracy plot between his own mother and brother! And didn't he come to his father later with repentant tears? And isn't God supposed to be the champion of the underdog? Father of forgiveness?

Well, God knew people like me would question this situation because he inspired Paul to write in Romans 9:11–16:

> Yet, before the twins were born or had done anything good
> or bad—in order that God's purpose in election might stand:

not by works but by him who calls—she was told, "The older will serve the younger." Just as it is written: "Jacob I loved, but Esau I hated." What then shall we say? Is God unjust? Not at all! For he says to Moses, "I will have mercy on whom I have mercy, and I will have compassion on whom I have compassion." It does not, therefore, depend on human desire or effort, but on God's mercy.

Although we are called to control ourselves and take action that aligns with God's will, it is through no means of our own that we can gain the Lord's favor. We must accept it as a free gift. Whether at this stage in life you feel more like Jacob or Esau, the important thing to remember is that you have something neither of them had . . . the atoning blood of Jesus over you. You are the recipient of the free gift of life through him. So why fight to do anything but control yourself and yield to what God wants to give you?

Back to Esau. When you examine his reaction, you realize he wasn't really the underdog. It wasn't really with a repentant heart that he wept. A repentant heart recognizes the error of its ways and turns the opposite direction in surrender. He begged and pleaded, but then when he didn't get his way, he went so far as to plot to kill his brother!

But I think the bigger picture here is that God will bless whom he will bless, and any attempt on our part to thwart or circumvent this by our own will is futile. God is love and wishes to give us his best. Resting in that fact takes the burden off our shoulders and places it on him to provide. In order to do this, we must continually be engaging in behaviors governed by surrender to his will. We must learn self-control lest we sell our hearts and lives for a meal that will just leave us hungry.

Conversation Starters/Reflection Questions: **Self-Control**

1. Name five areas of your life over which you feel you tend to lose control. (Example: controlling your tongue)

2. Of those five, which one do you struggle with the most? Why?

3. Is lack of self-control a sin? Give a Scripture reference to support your answer.

4. Describe a time when you were able to wait for the Lord's provision, and the situation turned out to be better than what you could have manufactured for yourself. If you can't think of a time, write a prayer to God asking for enough self-control to wait for him in a current or upcoming situation.

5. If self-control is a fruit of the Spirit that you know you possess in abundance, how can you keep from becoming a "control freak"?

LOVE

Think about why your own self-control is an expression of love for your spouse. Write a letter to your spouse that reaffirms this thought.

DEPLOYMENT

You are half a world apart from your spouse. You are left to hold yourself accountable in a lot of ways. Out-of-control, reckless behavior likely won't be met with the same consequences it would be when you are not separated by deployment. But you need to realize now that lack of self-control, while perhaps not immediately confronted, will still impact your marriage. Identify specific areas of your personal life and marriage that, while usually aided by the presence of a spouse to be kept under control, will need to fall under the scrutiny of self-control during deployment. Discuss ways to hold each other accountable to trusting in God's provision while exercising self-control.

35

THOUGHTS

"Remember when life's path is steep to keep your mind even."

—Horace, *ancient Roman poet*

FAITH

Him: "Finally, brothers and sisters, whatever is true, whatever is noble, whatever is right, whatever is pure, whatever is lovely, whatever is admirable—if anything is excellent or praiseworthy—think about such things" (Phil. 4:8).

Her: "You will keep in perfect peace those whose minds are steadfast, because they trust in you" (Isa. 26:3).

HOPE

Every action begins with a thought. Praise God, not every thought becomes an action! Can you imagine the chaos on the highway alone if we allowed every road rage-induced thought to produce the vindictive action we envision in our minds? Second Corinthians 10:5 says, "We demolish arguments and every pretension that sets itself up against the knowledge of God, and we take captive every thought to make it obedient to Christ." Why is that important? Let's use God's beautiful creation, our imaginations, to think about the answer to that question.

Picture the world's largest Jumbotron projecting to a vast audience. The audience is made up of people like Billy Graham, the pope, and your sweet, elderly grandmother who still thinks "darn" is a curse word. It might also include your spouse, your boss, and the ultimate guest . . . Jesus himself. Now, imagine they are all seated comfortably in a huge arena and are curious as to what they are about to see.

The lights dim and a series of silent scenes begin to play. The scenes are your thoughts. The first is the one you had when the careless teen-ager cut you off on the way home from work. In that scene, instead of swerving to avoid a collision, you swerve toward him and send him over the embankment. The next scene is from earlier that same day. You were on your lunch break and sitting in the common area in which your co-workers tend to congregate . . . including the really hot red-head you've noticed more than once. Now remember, this didn't really happen, but what is shown on the screen is what went through your mind as she bent over to retrieve her lunch from the fridge.

You pat yourself on the back as you see that you managed to catch that thought before it escalated into something more. Sure, you should have walked away the moment she came in, and instead you chose to ignore your wife's call during your lunch break and hang around until the redhead left. But they were just thoughts, right? So what if they left you frustrated and irritable. At least you didn't act on them, you reason to yourself.

Several more scenes pass. Some scenes are beautiful and peace-ful. During your quiet time that morning, your thoughts were serene, and you started the day with your mind focused on the Lord. What happened between then and the road rage? You failed to take every thought captive.

The screen goes black. When it lights up again, your thoughts are no longer the ones on the screen. It's your wife's thoughts that are there.

You look to where she had been sitting, but she's gone. You try to focus as her show starts. Her day began much as yours did . . . with thoughts of surrendering the chaos of the day to her Heavenly Father. But then you are shocked by what you see next. She too is thinking of you and your co-worker in the break room. Your wife is in the middle of a difficult situation with the ringing phone in her hand, imagining a scene that makes your dear grandmother gasp and nearly faint. It dawns on you that your failure to take your thoughts captive—even though you didn't actually act on them—had an effect on your decisions, on those you care about, and even on their thoughts.

Now, I'm not trying to pick on men. The wife in this scenario is just as guilty of letting her thoughts control her. Instead of taking her difficult situation to the Lord first, she turns to her husband. When she looks for solutions and peace in him and can't get it, she allows her fear to corrode her thought life.

The mind is a very powerful thing. Out of all of God's creations, we are the only ones to whom he gave the ability to reason and imagine. Our minds are capable of things that no other creature on the planet can conceive. But don't for a moment underestimate the gravity of what that means. With it comes great responsibility.

This little short story from my crazy brain might seem far-fetched to you. But Jesus doesn't need a Jumbotron to know our every thought. Psalm 139:2 says, "You know when I sit and when I rise; you perceive my thoughts from afar." Are we crucifying him every day for what he sees there? Trust him to purify you by the renewing of your mind.

Conversation Starters/Reflection Questions: **Thoughts**

1. How do you take every thought captive?

2. Do you think men or women struggle the most with controlling their thought life? Why?

3. What are you allowing to influence your thoughts?

4. Are less-than-wholesome thoughts sin if you don't act on them? Why or why not?

5. How active is your imagination? What are some good ways to channel that creativity into something edifying to your Lord and your marriage?

LOVE

Use your creative and active imagination to write a letter to your spouse that will make him or her blush. Yep, I said it. There's no need to get X-rated. Your spouse can fill in the blanks with his or her own thoughts of you.

DEPLOYMENT

Keeping your marriage exciting and both spouses fulfilled during deployment is extremely challenging. And for many couples, the comfort level of discussing this type of topic is very low. So I'm going to open the discussion for you. Forgive me if I make you uncomfortable, but so many friends have shared with me that this was something they dealt with during deployment that I'm willing to make you squirm a little.

Pornography, masturbation, and even fantasizing are taboo to speak of but serious discussions you need to have. While pornography is thought by most Christians to be a sin, there are several schools of thought on what is sinful as far as masturbation is concerned. Dr. James Dobson and Dr. Gary Chapman are two authors who have given their opinions on this subject. I urge you to research these topics together as a couple.

My husband and I attended a marriage conference on base in Germany and heard Dr. Gary Chapman address this issue. His biggest takeaway was concerning the thought process involved. If masturbation was agreed upon by the couple, it was to occur only under the provision that the spouse be the only image in the mind. I would caution that most people lack the mental self-control not to let their minds wander when presented with the temptation. And some of you may disagree with the idea altogether.

Regardless of where you land in your discussions, the important thing is to have them. Don't be embarrassed to speak to your spouse about this. You might not think it is an issue. Even if it isn't, you will have grown in intimacy merely through the conversation. Pray about this together. Ask God to direct your decisions and beseech him to allow all thoughts and actions to be beneficial to your marriage and, most of all, glorifying to him.

36

ANGER

"I found hope when you found me.
And your love grew angry
so sin won't claim what is yours . . . "

—Tyler Krause, *lyrics from "I Found Hope"*

FAITH

Him: "People with good sense restrain their anger" (Prov. 19:11a NLT 1996).

Her: "Be angry, and *yet* do not sin; do not let the sun go down on your anger" (Eph. 4:26 NASB).

HOPE

You know the feeling. Hot blush paints your face. Your mind swirls with questions of why and where is the justice. Your heart takes on a rapid pace, and the blood coursing through your veins feels about to boil over. It's anger.

So many things have been written on how to manage it or even rid yourself of it altogether. But to say that anger—or any emotion, for that matter—has no place in us is saying that God made a mistake when he created us . . . that there is something misplaced in his intelligent design. Now, it is true that sin and the fallen nature of humanity has skewed and blown out of proportion the way this very powerful emotion was intended to function. But anger in its primal form is very useful.

Let's look at the example of Jesus in the temple. In his day, pilgrims journeyed to the temple to offer their sacrifices for Passover. Many who traveled a great distance bought an animal there in the temple courtyard instead of bringing an animal with them. I imagine this had become a very lucrative business. Think along the lines of ticket scalpers at a sporting event. Also, there was apparently a tax for entrance into the temple, and the money changers were exchanging foreign currency . . . no doubt with interest added for the service. All this took place in Jesus' father's house. Of course he felt compelled to defend both God and the temple.

Mark 11:15–17 reads:

> On reaching Jerusalem, Jesus entered the temple courts and began driving out those who were buying and selling there. He overturned the tables of the money changers and the benches of those selling doves, and would not allow anyone to carry merchandise through the temple courts. And as he taught them, he said, "Is it not written: 'My house will be called a house of prayer for all nations'? But you have made it 'a den of robbers.'"

The anger he displayed is often called "righteous indignation." He was angry that his father's house and acts of worship were being exploited for profit. But his reaction of overturning the money changers' tables and scattering the animals that were being sold shows that he was angry at the sin . . . not the sinner. And verse 17 says "as he taught them." Even in his anger, Jesus was looking out for the welfare of those who were sinning. He wanted to use his anger to help them see the error of their ways and condemn their sin, not they themselves. If Jesus had walked up to a money changer and punched him in the face, his anger would have caused him to sin. But that was far from what he did.

So often our anger becomes a problem because it is accompanied by rage and a prideful need to defend ourselves; therefore, we leave no room for God's wrath instead of ours. The memory verse in Ephesians this week implores us to be angry, yet not sin. We are naturally going to rail against the injustices of the world. We are supposed to defend those who cannot defend themselves. Psalm 82:3 says, "Defend the cause of the weak and fatherless; maintain the rights of the poor and oppressed" (NIV 1984). We are not, however, called to be the jury, judge, and executioner of justice.

"If it is possible, as far as it depends on you, live at peace with everyone. Do not take revenge, my dear friends, but leave room for God's wrath, for it is written: 'It is mine to avenge; I will repay,' says the Lord. On the contrary: 'If your enemy is hungry, feed him; if he is thirsty, give him something to drink. In doing this, you will heap burning coals on his head'" (Rom. 12:18–20).

Anger exists to let us know that a boundary has been breached. Andy Stanley says that where there is anger, somewhere in the equation is a hurting person or a person sympathetic to a hurt being inflicted.[8] Our energies would be much better spent rooting out the source of the hurt and pointing the hurting person to the Healer.

Conversation Starters/Reflection Questions: **Anger**

1. Why do you think anger tends to be a default emotion for so many people?

2. How likely are you to respond in anger and inflict wrath when conflict occurs? Why do you think that is?

3. What makes you angry?

4. What are some ways you can manage anger and possibly even teach in the midst of it?

5. Have you ever been the victim of someone else's anger? Describe how it made you feel and the outcome of the situation.

LOVE

Write a letter to your spouse apologizing for any times when you have responded in anger. Make a promise to do your best to handle all conflict with love. Contemplate your desire to protect your spouse and write about what you feel in that regard.

DEPLOYMENT

So many "injustices" are confronted during deployment. Downrange, you will encounter things that your mind probably never thought possible. You will want to respond in anger at harm inflicted on innocent people... your brothers and sisters in arms and perhaps the indigenous people. A temptation will be to bring your own wrath. On the home front, there are countless opportunities to become righteously indignant over the unfairness of separation. Devise a plan for "leaving room for the Lord's vindication" instead of your own. When you feel yourself getting angry, stop and pray for the Lord to show you what boundary breech occurred, help you distill the source of the anger, and submit it all to him.

If you find that anger is truly a struggle you cannot overcome, seek professional help. Several resources are available through the military and church communities. Your local chaplain can easily point you in the right direction to get the help and encouragement you need.

37

EVANGELISM

"Christianity is one beggar telling another beggar where he found bread."

—D. T. Niles, *Ceylonese priest and evangelist*

FAITH

Him: "Therefore go and make disciples of all nations, baptizing them in the name of the Father and of the Son and of the Holy Spirit, and teaching them to obey everything I have commanded you. And surely I am with you always, to the very end of the age" (Matt. 28:19–20).

Her: "And I pray that the sharing of your faith may become effective for the full knowledge of every good thing that is in us for the sake of Christ" (Philem. 1:6 esv).

HOPE

"Heather, get up off the floor. We're going to meet a friend of mine for lunch."

On the last day of Erica's visit, I was lying on the floor in my pajamas, and it was getting close to noon. But she might as well have asked me to give birth to an alien. There was no way I was going anywhere, least of all to meet a high-ranking officer's wife at the Air Force Academy. I'm not completely certain . . . it might have been that I felt guilty for the way I had treated her during her stay, or it could have been that she was literally kicking my butt to get me off the floor. Regardless, she somehow got me up and dressed, and soon I found myself sitting at the kitchen table with not one but two women I had never met.

As I sat with those women, all I could do was tell the story. The story of David's death, my newfound single parenthood, and a faith that was dim at that moment but somehow a beacon of hope. And despite myself, God was being glorified just by my being willing to open my mouth and speak his name. It was then that I started having the inkling that sharing the story God had given me, my testimony and the good news of Jesus, was not only therapeutic to me, but God-ordained.

> But in your hearts revere Christ as Lord. Always be prepared to give an answer to everyone who asks you to give the reason for the hope that you have. But do this with gentleness and respect, keeping a clear conscience, so that those who speak maliciously against your good behavior in Christ may be ashamed of their slander. (1 Pet. 3:15–16)

So I sat there and gave the reason for the hope I had in the midst of wallowing in my own sorrow. I have always felt that God has a sense of humor. At the very least, I'm convinced that with or without us on board, he enjoys using unforeseen avenues for accomplishing a plan we couldn't orchestrate if we tried. That day would prove to be the beginning of him rewriting my life story.

One of those women turned out to be the wife of the Academy commander. She was hosting a group of key spouses that night and insisted I stay and speak to them. That night's meeting led to my speaking to hundreds of people in the Academy auditorium on the three-month anniversary of my husband's death. I told my audience that everyone has a story to share, and everyone can find God in their story if they are just willing to look for him. I left them with Isaiah 6:8: "The Lord said, 'Whom shall I send?' And I said, 'Here I am Lord, send me.'" It was my husband's life verse. It was becoming mine.

As I stood chatting with people afterward, a man approached me. His eyes were steely and he was clearly resolved. He proceeded to inform me that he was an atheist and disagreed with everything I had said. He assured me that he didn't need God in order to be resilient and that he was surprised they had let me speak there. I have to admit it was difficult to hear. But I told him I appreciated his honesty and that I had only one request of him . . . that he seek for himself what I had spoken of. That if he sought the Lord and found nothing, then what did he have to lose? I don't know exactly how the conversation concluded, but others were approaching, and at some point I no longer saw him in the crowd.

I prayed for that man continually from then on. Over the next nine months, I did twenty-three more events . . . I spoke to thousands of people in three countries, all because God gave me a story to tell. At times, I have asked myself why. In the dark moments, I have questioned why I kept putting myself out there for people like that atheist to knock down. It was in one of those doubtful moments that I begged God to remind me why we are called to praise him and share the gospel when life seems so hard. Nearly a year after I spoke at the Academy, God gave me an answer.

I was sitting on the side of the road. I had just run into a guard rail and was steaming mad (at myself for trying to mess with my phone while driving). I drove down to the nearest gas station so I could get out and check on my car. As I pulled into the parking lot, I got a call from my babysitter.

"I've been meaning to tell you something really cool that happened."

I put the phone on Bluetooth (something I should have done to begin with), got out, and assessed the damage to my Jeep. Thankfully, there was no damage, but my day had been shaken up regardless.

"Please tell me everyone is okay, Gillian."

"Yeah, we're all good. So, I was working at the coffee shop the other day, and this guy came in wearing a shirt with Isaiah 6:8 on it. I commented on it, and you're never going to guess what he said!"

By this point, she had my full attention. I got back in the Jeep but sat in the parking lot.

"He told me that he had only recently gotten the shirt when he became a believer in Christ. That he used to be an atheist until he heard this war widow speak at the Academy, and he decided to seek for himself the God she had spoken of. I asked if he remembered your name and he did and I started crying as I told him I babysit for you! Isn't that so cool?!"

It was beyond cool. It was just one example of the way God's Word never returns void. No matter how broken the vessel that carries the light, it will shine through the cracks. And actually, the more broken that vessel is, the more light you see. God was gracious enough to show me the good that he allows to come from our bad situations.

Someone told me recently that God only gives stories to those willing to tell them. Evangelism is a fancy word for telling God's story in your life. You might not feel like the storyteller type. But you have a story to tell. God has given you everything you need to be a witness for him. You might feel sometimes like God is giving you a bigger story than you'd like. Or maybe you don't feel like your story is one worth telling. But his is.

If we think the purpose for our being on this earth is for our own satisfaction and gain, we will forever be disappointed and never able to discern the will of God for our lives. The will of God for our lives, the purpose of life, is to bring God glory. And he is always glorified when his story is told.

Conversation Starters/Reflection Questions: **Evangelism**

1. Define lifestyle witness.

2. Why is sharing the gospel of Jesus and the work he's done in your life so important as a Christian?

3. How likely are you to share your faith with others in your workplace and community? Why?

4. How did you come to know the Lord? Where would you be if no one had ever shared or encouraged the gospel in your life both before and after conversion?

5. What are some practical ways you can live out your faith and share your story?

LOVE

Sometimes we can't love every single little thing about our spouse. But we should always be able to love the Christ we see in them. Write a letter that praises your spouse for the lifestyle witness he or she is to you.

DEPLOYMENT

With everything having to be politically correct these days, particularly in the military, evangelism can be a bit of a gray area. But you can always share your personal story. Talk through your testimony with your spouse. Some key points to think about including in your story are who you were before Jesus, how you came to know him, who you are since giving your life to him, and things he's done in your life. Pray together that God will present opportunities for you to share your story with those who need to hear it. Deployment is a difficult time and people recognize that. Be prepared to give an answer for your hope during this time.

38

CONTENTMENT

"Much of our happiness depends less on our circumstances and more on our attitude."

—Martha Washington, *wife of the first U.S. President*

FAITH

Him: "But godliness with contentment is great gain, for we brought nothing into the world, and we cannot take anything out of the world. But if we have food and clothing, with these we will be content" (1 Tim. 6:6–8 ESV).

Her: "For the sake of Christ, then, I am content with weaknesses, insults, hardships, persecutions, and calamities. For when I am weak, then I am strong" (2 Cor. 12:10 ESV).

HOPE

"Bloom where you're planted." These were the words she gave me when I asked the squadron commander's wife for one piece of advice. It was our very first assignment since marriage and my husband's first assignment after commissioning. I had no idea how to thrive in a lifestyle wrought with hardship from separation, imminent danger, frequent upheaval, and expectations I couldn't understand. But it has proven to be the most valuable lesson I have learned from being a military spouse: contentment.

Contentment does not equal having everything you want. It means having peace in your heart when you don't get what you want. It means rejoicing in all circumstances. It is marked by thankfulness being your first reaction to blessings. It means that God is firmly rooted as the center of your existence and that his presence alone sustains you.

Be careful not to assume that you can engineer a contented heart by suppressing your true desires to the point that you can fake being happy. True contentment is a complete surrender to the Lord—it's a trust that where you are and what you've been given are exactly what you need because you trust the One who gave them to you. Job said, "The Lord giveth and the Lord taketh away" (1:21). We also should recognize that all we strive so hard to possess is only held on to by the grace of the One who gave it.

When we learn that true joy comes from the Lord alone, we recognize that happiness is based on circumstances and that we should desire joy far more. A heart that is content can dwell in this state of being regardless of outlying circumstances because the calm, the peace, and the joy lie within. There is joy in salvation (Ps. 51:12), the joy of the Lord is strength (Neh. 8:10), and though sorrow may last through the night, joy comes in the morning (Ps. 30:5). The common denominator is that joy comes from the Lord.

Jesus isn't going to say, "Well done, my good and faithful servant" because you had great things or because you achieved greatness. He's going to say, "Well done, my good and faithful servant" because you used what you were given, whether plentiful or very little, to do great things for him. If you determine in your heart to wait for something better to come along instead of making the best of what you're given, you run the risk of missing out on the joy that is right in front of you.

Paul said this of contentment while in prison: "I know what it is to be in need, and I know what it is to have plenty. I have learned the secret of being content in any and every situation, whether well fed or hungry, whether living in plenty or in want. I can do all this through him who gives me strength" (Phil. 4:12–13). I think the key word in that passage is *learned*. You have to experience something in order to truly learn it. You can read about the poor, but until you have tasted want and experienced poverty, you will never fully internalize their plight.

I have a friend who is a full-time missionary in Haiti. While I was staying with his family during a two-week trip to the country he and his family now call home, he told me that short-term missions do little to nothing for the impoverished. At first I railed at this statement. Then he went on to clarify. While the nature of most situations hinders short-term missions from making long-term impacts on the vast need, they are of invaluable benefit to the ones serving on the mission trip.

You cannot discern light without having been in darkness. An experience that changes the heart, whether for good or bad, will have longevity and impact. And your heart will be better for the experience. Paul was able to learn the secret of contentment because he knew that whether in plenty or in want, the key was Christ. He knew that all his soul needed to truly be satisfied was a relationship with the Lord. A relationship that placed all desires, all circumstances, all provision in the hands of the One who created him and everything around him.

Contentment comes when you can look around you . . . at the people in your life, the things you possess, the roles you play, and the place in which you find yourself . . . and, regardless of what you see, you choose to say, "It is well with my soul."

Conversation Starters/Reflection Questions: **Contentment**

1. On a scale of 1 to 10, how content are you in each of these areas?
   a. Relationship with the Lord
   b. Your marriage
   c. Your current job assignment/duties/role you play
   d. Your finances
   e. Yourself

2. What can you do to cultivate contentment in the area in which you scored the lowest?

3. How does contentment in plenty or in want seem countercultural?

4. How certain are you that the Lord is the author of all things? Are you resting in his authority? Why or why not?

5. Why do you think we are so fascinated with "Cinderella" stories?

LOVE

Over time, we begin to take our spouse for granted. We sometimes even begin to think that we aren't satisfied with the spouse God gave us. But Malachi encourages us to be faithful to the love of our youth (2:13–16). Write a letter of encouragement to your spouse in which you remind him or her of all the ways you know he or she is the one for you and why you are more than content with the love of your life.

DEPLOYMENT

Sometimes the "grass is greener" mentality kicks into high gear during deployment. We tend to think if we just got out of the military, got out of this marriage, got out of our yard and into the greener one, then everything would get better. But we are called to be content even when the grass in our yard looks more like a moonscape.

One of the ways I overcame my discontent during deployment was to do everything possible to embrace it instead of fighting it. Work together to channel your negative energy about deployment into a positive outlook. Doing devotions like this one together is a great step toward learning to find contentment in every situation, and not only survive it but grow and benefit from it. When you finish this book, find another to work through together as a couple.

Stay focused on the blessings that come from every situation, and you are more likely to be able to "bloom where you're planted."

39

LOVE

"I have found the paradox, that if you love until it hurts,
there can be no more hurt, only more love.

—Mother Teresa, *Roman Catholic saint*

FAITH

Him: "Don't just pretend to love others. Really love them. Hate what is wrong. Hold tightly to what is good" (Rom. 12:9 NLT).

Her: "Place me like a seal over your heart, like a seal on your arm; for love is as strong as death, its jealousy unyielding as the grave. It burns like blazing fire, like a mighty flame. Many waters cannot quench love; rivers cannot sweep it away" (Song of Songs 8:6–7a).

HOPE

I will tell you up front that I'm not going to address the topic of love in the way you might expect in a couple's devotional. I could address the difference between the way men and women express love. I could address God's immense love for you and your marriage. Or I could address the way you should love your children no matter how rebellious they are or how frustrated they make you. Instead, I feel the Lord has placed on my heart to write about love in a way that is, honestly, new to me and I would venture to say, somewhat foreign to most of us.

I don't want to equate myself with one of the patriarchs of the faith, but to steal an expression from what Jacob experienced: I have been wrestling with God. I come to my computer sore from the experience. But just like any good workout, the soreness reminds me of the effort put forth. Anything worth having is worth struggling for. So fasten your seatbelt and ask the Lord to open your mind and heart to a concept that might not feel as good as the Valentine's Day love to which we are accustomed.

In my quiet time this morning I found myself in 1 John. It was comforting . . . "true love knows no fear" . . . but it was 2 John that resonated with me in a new way. Verse 6: "And this is love: that we walk in obedience to his commands. As you have heard from the beginning, his command is that you walk in love."

So my next question was, "Where, exactly, do I struggle to walk in love?" There are the obvious places . . . I struggle to walk in love when my children disobey me or misbehave. I struggle when I put unfair expectations on friends and family and then feel let down when they can't deliver. (I want to stress the word *unfair*; I have amazing friends and family.) But the real revelation came in what I learned next.

Having identified all my areas of weakness (or so I thought), I turned to Romans. It's a great place to go when you are rebuked and need a good encouragement to follow up. I landed in Romans 8:37–39, "No, in all these things we are more than conquerors through him who loved us. For I am convinced that neither death nor life, neither angels nor demons, neither the present nor the future, nor any powers, neither height nor depth, nor anything else in all creation, will be able to separate us from the love of God that is in Christ Jesus our Lord."

While this is a great passage to reiterate that God's love is so immense nothing can separate his children from it, it was something across the page that brought me to my knees. Romans 9:15 reads: "For he says to Moses, 'I will have mercy on whom I have mercy, and I will have compassion on whom I have compassion.'" Now, you might be wondering where the connection is. I was, too, at first. What could this possibly have to do with the lesson I was certain I had nailed down? Love. Walk in love; nothing can separate us from God's love. Then it hit me. I don't get to choose whom I am called to love. Or who will love me in return.

Verses 20–22 say:

> But who are you, a human being, to talk back to God? "Shall what is formed say to him who formed it, 'Why did you make me like this?'" Does not the potter have the right to make out of the same lump of clay some pottery for special purposes and some for common use? What if God, although choosing to show his wrath and make his power known, bore with great patience the objects of his wrath—prepared for destruction?

Could it be? Some creations, to include those made in the image of God, could be formed solely for the purpose of destruction? My heart thumped a panic rhythm. Surely David wasn't created just so he could die? But aren't we all heading toward that end at some point? Maybe these verses were meant to tell me that the man who killed David was created for the purpose of destruction. Sounds callous. But that assumption seemed easier to grasp. After all, didn't God intentionally harden the hearts of people like Pharaoh and Saul for the purpose of bringing about his plan? When in doubt, keep reading.

Verses 23–25: "What if he did this to make the riches of his glory known to the objects of his mercy, whom he prepared in advance for glory—even us, whom he also called, not only from the Jews but also from the Gentiles? As he says in Hosea: 'I will call them "my people" who are not my people; and I will call her "my loved one" who is not my loved one.'"

It doesn't matter who we think are the ones intended for noble purposes, common use, or destruction. The bottom line is we were all created from the same lump of clay.

I am called to walk in love . . . loving all people. Even those who wish me and my people harm. I didn't even realize I was harboring resentment toward the Afghan people. When they returned from deployment, I spoke to David's men about letting go of any bitterness they might have had about David's death, mainly because I don't want anyone choosing not to have a personal relationship with the Lord because he or she isn't able to make sense of what happened. But I had no idea there was a seed of disdain in my own heart.

I know I have forgiven the person who took his own life and, in the process, the lives of my husband and three others. But today I realized that is not all I'm called to do.

Forgiveness means nothing if we don't change the landscape of our hearts afterward. I am called to love my enemy. And until my husband was killed, I don't think I ever really even understood the term "enemy." But 1 Corinthians 13 tells us that the greatest command is love. Could it be that God inspired these words because he knew to really love—in the true, unselfish sense of the word; when there is nothing gained in return—would be one of the most challenging commands he would give us? I think so.

So I'll finish my thoughts back where I started in 2 John 8: "Watch out that you do not lose what we have worked for, but that you may be rewarded fully." The reward comes in obeying the command to love. Learn to love in a new way, the right way, and it's impossible to lose everything. Why? Because "now these three remain: faith, hope and love. But the greatest of these is love" (1 Cor. 13:13). Now, walk in that love.

Conversation Starters/Reflection Questions: **Love**

1. What do you think it means to love the right way? Is there a wrong way to love someone?

2. Gary Chapman in *The Five Love Languages* says that each person gives and receives love in one of five ways: Acts of Service, Gifts, Words of Affirmation, Physical Touch, or Quality Time.[9] Identify and discuss with your spouse the primary way you express your love and the primary way you feel loved by someone.

3. What makes someone lovable? Is there a person (or people) you are struggling to love?

4. How is love for each other different than the love you give to others?

5. What do you think is the difference between romantic love and covenant love? Which is more important to have in a marriage? Are they equally important?

LOVE

Finally, the classic love letter. Write a letter to your spouse expressing how much you love him or her. Recall the reasons you chose this person out of all the other people in the world. Remind your spouse of what you love about him or her physically, spiritually, emotionally, and practically. Promise that your love will stand the test of time. Remember, you are the only one who will love your spouse in this way . . . do it well.

DEPLOYMENT

Loving others during deployment can be challenging. We are called to love not only those who love us, but our enemies as well. That's tough to swallow when you or your loved one is fighting a war. What does walking in love during deployment mean to you? Think about and discuss whether there are ways you need to better love those you are defending, both at home and abroad, and those you consider your enemies. Pray that God would make room in your heart to love as he loves us.

While on the topic of love, talk through how well you are loving each other. What practical things (gifts, words of affirmation, and so on) might be missing from the equation during this time of separation? Renew your vows to one another via FaceTime or phone conversation. Continually be looking for opportunities to love on each other. And always, always, let "I love you" be the last words your spouse hears from you.

40

PERSEVERANCE AND REINTEGRATION

"It matters less how well you run the race . . .
just finish strong."

—David Gray; *loving husband and father, KIA 8/8/12*

FAITH

Him: "Blessed is the man who perseveres under trial, because when he has stood the test, he will receive the crown of life that God has promised to those who love him" (James 1:12 NIV 1984).

Her: "Because you have kept My command to persevere, I also will keep you from the hour of trial which shall come upon the whole world, to test those who dwell on the earth" (Rev. 3:10 NKJV).

HOPE

I was completely exhausted. David had finally convinced me to run a 5K with him. You are probably laughing at the fact that 3.1 miles had left me feeling utterly drained and flat worn out. But truth is truth . . . I was over it. He, bearing the nickname of PT Ninja, could have orbited me the entire time. But, being the loving man he was, he had run (okay, at a thirteen-minute mile, walked) my pace. Pregnant women pushing double jogging strollers had been passing me. To say I am not an athletic person would be an understatement.

I could see the finish line ahead of me. I slowed to a near snail's pace and gave my husband a frustrated look.

"Can I please just walk the rest of the way? I did what you wanted and participated. I'm done."

He wrapped his arm around my waist and pulled me to him.

"You can walk if you want to. It matters less how well you run the race, but you'll feel better if you finish strong. Just finish strong."

I rolled my eyes at him, and because I have a tendency to be a smart aleck, I sprinted across the finish line without warning so that I could say I beat him in a race. When it was over, he wrapped his arms around me in a big hug, and I knew in the end I had made him proud.

I thought little of his words that day until I was at the tree line on Pikes Peak nearly two years later. I had planned on making the climb on August 11th as an anniversary present to David. But on that day, I had been flying back from receiving his body at Dover Air Force Base. So on August 30, 2012, six days after I buried my husband at Arlington National Cemetery, I was two miles from completing the half marathon climb to the summit. Once again, I found myself exhausted and lacking the motivation to persevere. It was then I heard his words echo in my heart . . . finish strong.

We are called to "run with perseverance the race marked out for us" (Heb. 12:1). Sometimes it feels like we are being asked to do the impossible. But take comfort in knowing you serve a God who is steadfast. He never changes. And he asks us to trust him and walk by faith, not by sight.

Before I had LASIK surgery, I was extremely nearsighted. I could see fairly well up close. But when my gaze turned beyond what was right in front of me, everything grew hazy. How like that we tend to be.

We tend to focus on the seeming impossibility of overcoming what lies ahead and, in the process, trip over God's provision that is right before us. In the blur of our finite vision sits a mountain on the horizon. We fret over how we could ever be expected to climb it. But the Lord has equipped us to see what we need to see, to do what is required of us right now, and to trust him with the future. And how often do we realize on the other side of an obstacle that it wasn't as large as we perceived it to be? Sometimes it turns out that the mountain on the horizon, the one we spent so much time fretting over, is not a mountain at all. Or maybe we get there and it is indeed a mountain. It is treacherous and uncharted and there is no way around it. In those moments, believe that the Creator of that mountain will serve as your guide if you just keep your eyes on him. All he asks is that we persevere.

So tilt your head to the sky and cry out to the Lord for strength. Never give up. Live and love with a passion. Never take a moment of the journey for granted. And rest in the assurance that "he who began a good work in you will carry it on to completion until the day of Christ Jesus" (Phil. 1:6).

Conversation Starters/Reflection Questions: **Perseverance and Reintegration**

1. What motivates you to persevere?

2. Why does it sometimes feel like giving up is the best option?

3. If you could do anything you wanted without fear and without worry of growing weary, what would you do? What's stopping you?

4. Describe a time when you persevered through hardship and it paid off.

5. Why do you think you'll feel better if you finish strong?

LOVE

No one has the ability to motivate and inspire your spouse like you do.
Write a letter encouraging him or her to run the race with perseverance.

DEPLOYMENT

You've made it. You've persevered through deployment. But seeing it through to completion doesn't stop when the welcome home sign comes down. Reintegration can be a difficult time for some families. Be sensitive to the changes in your spouse, his or her routine, and so on when readjusting to an intact family unit. Take advantage of the reintegration services that are available through your local installation. Talk about the reality of PTSD and be open to getting help if you or your spouse needs it. Keep communication open. Be patient with one another. Persevere. Finish strong.

RESOURCES

ANGER
Stanley, Andy. *Enemies of the Heart: Breaking Free from the Four Emotions That Control You.* Colorado Springs: Multnomah Books, 2011.

BOREDOM
"10 Tips from Bible Verses on How to Stop Being Lazy." *Bible-Verses-Insights.com.* June 10, 2009. http://bible-verses-insights.com/2009/06/how-to-stop-being-lazy.

BOUNDARIES
Cloud, Dr. Henry and Dr. John Townsend. *Boundaries: When to Say Yes, How to Say No to Take Control of Your Life.* Grand Rapids: Zondervan, 1992.

CHILDREN
Sesame Street DVD *Talk, Listen, Connect* is available through:
    www.sesamestreet.org
    www.militaryonesource.mil
    www.uso.org

Daddy dolls and pillows with recordable voice boxes are available at www.daddydolls.com.

COMMUNICATION
Four Personality Types taken from Gary Chapman and Ramon L. Presson. 101 Conversation Starters for Couples. Chicago: Moody Publishers, 2012.

DEATH
Albom, Mitch. T*he Five People You Meet in Heaven.* New York City: Hyperion Publishers, 2006.

DISAPPOINTMENT
Zavada, Jack. "The Christian Response to Disappointment." *Religion & Spirituality.* About.com. Accessed February 25, 2014. http://christianity. about.com/od/singlesresources/a/disappointment.htm.

EXPECTATIONS
www.whattoexpect.com for books, blogs, and other resources.

FAILURE
Henry, Matthew. *The Zondervan NIV Matthew Henry Commentary: In One Volume.* Grand Rapids: Zondervan, 1992.

FINANCES
Budget-driven resources:
> **Dave Ramsey**
> www.daveramsey.com
>
> **Crown Financial Ministries**
> www.crown.org

Urgent needs:
> **Military One Source**
> www.militaryonesource.mil
>
> **Air Force Aid Society**
> www.afas.org
>
> **USAA Financial Services**
> www.usaa.com
>
> **Red Cross**
> www.redcross.org

HOPE
Henry, Matthew. *The Zondervan NIV Matthew Henry Commentary: In One Volume.* Grand Rapids: Zondervan, 1992.

LOVE
Chapman, Gary. *The Five Love Languages: The Secret to Love That Lasts.* Chicago: Northfield Publishing, 2009.

ENDNOTES

[1] Henry Cloud and John Townsend, *Boundaries: When to Say Yes, How to Say No to Take Control of Your Life* (Grand Rapids: Zondervan Publishers, 1992), 27.

[2] Dave Ramsey, *Complete Guide to Money* (Brentwood, TN: Lampo Press, 2012), 22.

[3] Gary Chapman and Ramon L. Presson, *101 Conversation Starters for Couples* (Chicago: Moody Publishers, 2012).

[4] Mitch Albom, *The Five People You Meet in Heaven* (New York: Hyperion Books, 2006), 173.

[5] Jack Zavada, "The Christian Response to Disappointment," *Religion & Spirituality, About.com,* accessed February 25, 2014, http://christianity.about.com/od/singlesresources/a/disappointment.htm.

[6] Matthew Henry, Zondervan *NIV Matthew Henry Commentary: In One Volume* (Grand Rapids: Zondervan, 1992), 1024.

[7] Ibid., 595.

[8] Andy Stanley, *Enemies of the Heart: Breaking Free from the Four Emotions That Control You* (Colorado Springs: Multnomah Books, 2011).

[9] Gary Chapman, *The Five Love Languages: The Secret to Love That Lasts* (Chicago: Northfield Publishing, 2009.)